Hiking
Oregon

by
Donna Lynn Ikenberry

(Formerly *The Hiker's Guide to Oregon*)

FALCON

Falcon Press® Publishing Co., Inc.,
Helena, Montana

A FALCON GUIDE

Falcon Press is continually expanding its list of recreational guidebooks. All books include detailed descriptions, accurate maps, and all the information necessary for enjoyable trips. You can order extra copies of this book and get information and prices for other Falcon guidebooks by writing Falcon Press, P.O. Box 1718, Helena, MT 59624 or calling toll-free 1-800-582-2665. Also, please ask for a free copy of our current catalog.

Photos by the author.
Cover Photo: Upper Multnomah Falls, Columbia River Gorge,
by David Jensen

Text pages printed on recycled paper

CAUTION

Outdoor recreational activities are by their very nature potentially hazardous. All participants in such activities must assume the responsibility for their own actions and safety. The information contained in this guidebook cannot replace sound judgment and good decision–making skills, which help reduce risk exposure, nor does the scope of this book allow for disclosure of all the potential hazards and risks involved in such activities.

Learn as much as possible about the outdoor recreational activities you participate in, prepare for the unexpected, and be safe and cautious. The reward will be a safer and more enjoyable experience.

For my parents

ACKNOWLEDGMENTS

As with each and every project I pursue, I must first give thanks to God for it is He who leads me safely along the various trails of life.

I thank God each day for my family, a constant source of inspiration and loving support. I am extremely proud of my parents, Beverly Bruer Ikenberry and Donald Ikenberry, to whom this book is dedicated. I am grateful to them and to my brother, Don Ikenberry, who is more than just a brother. He and my future "sister" Yolie are great pals, too. In addition, I want to thank all of my special friends who constantly shower me with their love and support. I also have to mention my Samoyed dog, Sam, who hiked two thousand miles with me before going "home" to dog heaven.

All of those at the USDA Forest Service, Bureau of Land Management, Oregon State Parks Department, and other agencies who gave of their time also deserve some recognition and a sincere "thank you."

I'm especially grateful for Stephanie Hakanson, a Klamath Falls, Ore., photographer and friend who so diligently prints my black and white photographs.

There are several outdoor companies—Avocet, Danner, Kelty, and Performance—that I must thank. My Avocet Vertech has helped in keeping track of my elevation; my Danner boots are certainly the most comfortable I have ever worn; my Kelty Redwing is a must for all the camera gear I lug around; and my tiny backpacking/bicycling tent has safely sheltered me from many a storm.

Lastly, my thanks wouldn't be complete without acknowledging Randall Green, guidebook editor, and Ric Bourie, reprint editor, at Falcon Press.

CONTENTS

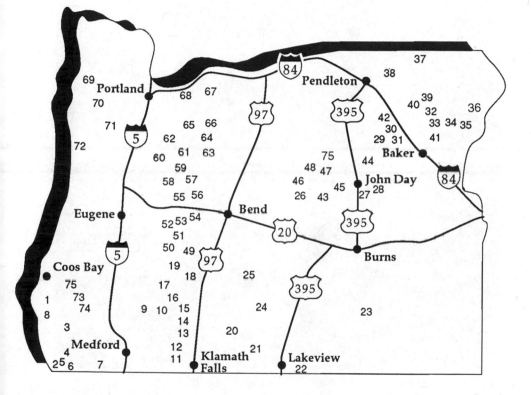

Author and her dog hiking East Eagle Trail No. 1910 to Hidden Lake.

HIKING IN OREGON, AN INTRODUCTION

Oregon is a hiker's paradise, a virtual potpourri of scenes to see, feel, smell, hear, and admire.

Trails traverse Oregon's magnificent shoreline, where migrating whales blow, sea lions bark, and gulls hang suspended in the wind. Trails crisscross forested mountain slopes, offering sweeping vistas from various points in the Coast Range, the Klamath Mountains, the mighty Cascades and the rugged Wallowas. Atop the awesome Steens, there are views in all directions as trees are nonexistent, save for the junipers and aspen trees growing on the lower slopes. In the southeast, desert trails skirt lava tubes and weave through the sage, allowing one to explore a world where pronghorn play, and eagles soar on high.

Oregon's trails range from short paths, less than a mile in length, to longer trails such as the 2,400-mile Pacific Crest National Scenic Trail which extends from Mexico to Canada. Trails offered in this guide are of varying lengths, some short and easy, others of greater lengths, taking several days or so to complete. Hikes written with children in mind are an added bonus for those with tiny tots.

I've chosen trails that are uncrowded and lightly used for the most part, although I've added several "busy" paths due to their overwhelming scenic beauty. I must admit, I prefer solitude—hiking for days without ever seeing another soul sans a friend or two—but there are some places worth visiting even if they are a bit crowded. I just hike in for the day and skip the overnight trek as I am obviously doing less harm to the environment. And I choose to go on weekdays, or before or after the summer holidays, when crowds are few and I still have the chance to experience aloneness. You can do the same.

After spending six summers hiking and backpacking throughout the Beaver State, I am often asked if I have a favorite spot, one which stands out from the rest. Although it's difficult to pinpoint that one special place, some personal favorites include the Wild Rogue, Eagle Cap, Kalmiopsis, and Hells Canyon Wilderness Areas, and Steens Mountain. I've enjoyed hiking more than 1,800 miles of Oregon's trails and I must say I've found something fascinating about them all.

I guess that's no surprise, Oregon is a fascinating state. It is divided by the Cascade Mountains, the picturesque crest splitting the state into two very distinct sides—western and eastern Oregon. Opposites in nearly every way, the east sees a lot of sunshine and very little rain.

Although the mountains of eastern Oregon receive a considerable amount of snow, low relief areas usually collect only ten to fifteen inches of precipitation per year. Some areas receive even less. The Alvord Desert, for example, only sees seven inches of precipitation making this the driest spot in Oregon. On the west side, where the majority of the population lives, the climate is often wet and soggy, with about thirty-five to forty-five inches of rain dousing the Willamette Valley and 100 inches per year pelting the Coast Range.

Many of the hikes listed in this guide are located in the Cascade Range, a series of peaks stretching more than 600 miles from northern California on into Canada. Oregon's highest peaks are found here: Mt. Hood, 11,235 feet; Mt. Jefferson, 10,495 feet; and the Three Sisters, 10,358 feet, are the three highest.

Crater Lake National Park, Oregon's only national park, rests in the Cascade Mountains. Eons ago Mt. Mazama grew to an estimated 12,000 feet, massive eruptions of magma spewing forth to build the mighty mountain. When the mountain cooled, glaciers periodically masked its flanks, carving out the U-shaped valleys seen today. And then the climatic eruptions began.

About 6,800 years ago, the mountain emptied from within, magma shooting towards the heavens. Then it collapsed, leaving a vast bowl-shaped caldera in its place. Today, Mt. Mazama lies scattered over eight states and three Canadian provinces. Researchers claim that ash six inches deep covered more than 5,000 square miles. Ash lies fifty feet deep in the Pumice Desert, located in the northern part of the preserve.

When volcanic processes ceased and the caldera cooled, the lake filled with rain and snow. Crater Lake is nearly six miles wide and it is 1,932 feet deep, the seventh deepest lake in the world. Crater Lake is perhaps the most beautiful of all the lakes in the world; it certainly is the most stunning of the Cascade Lakes. The view from Mt. Scott (Hike 15) is striking, the intense blue lake commanding the scene.

You'll find trails in many other areas as well. There are several in the Klamath Mountains, a rugged range of very old mountains in southwest Oregon and northwest California, and in the Coast Range, a low-elevation range stretching from the Klamaths to the Columbia River.

The Blue Mountains region hosts a number of trails as well. Located in the northeast corner of the state, the region includes a series of mountains—the Ochoco, Strawberry, Greenhorn, Elkhorn, Wallowas, and the Blue Mountains on the Oregon/Washington border. Although all are worth visiting, the Wallowas and Elkhorns are perhaps the most impressive. Both provide high granite slopes where trees are stunted, vegetation sparse, and the views are neverending. The Eagle Cap Wilderness rests in the Wallowas, an abrupt range some people compare to the Swiss Alps. I hardly think the Swiss Alps could be more beautiful.

There are many trails in this region including three in the Eagle Cap Wilderness (see Hikes 32, 33, and 34), two at John Day Fossil Beds National Monument (see Hikes 47 and 48), and two (Hikes 35 and 36) in the world's "deepest canyon in low relief territory," according to the Guinness Book of World Records. The canyon plunges 7,900 feet from the top of Idaho's Seven Devils Mountains, to the Snake River, the dividing line between Oregon and Idaho.

Several trails exist in the Basin and Range Province. Actually a continuation of the Great Basin, the Basin and Range province joins nearly all of Nevada, and portions of Utah, California and Idaho in forming the more than 200,000 square mile Great Basin.

The highest point in this part of Oregon is Steens Mountain, 9,733 feet. Although winter snows accumulate to great depths on the Steens (Steens Mountain Loop Road doesn't open until July), the average rainfall is somewhere between seven and twelve inches per year at lower elevations. In other words, southeast Oregon is desert, and an awe-inspiring one at that.

Oregon's natural community is as diverse as its landscape. More than 400

Wildlife abounds in the Oregon backcountry.

species of birds are known to live in or visit the state. Some, like the American bald eagle, spend the winter here, flying in from other western states and Canada to join those pairs who reside in the state year-round. In doing so they form the largest concentration of wintering bald eagles in the lower 48 states. They do—with wings as wide as a man is tall—what many of us wish we could do. They soar on high.

More than fifty species of amphibians and reptiles call Oregon home as do many species of fish. Anglers enjoy the rewards of bountiful salmon and tasty fried trout.

Mammals are abundant although not always visible. A quiet hiker may be able to see elk grazing in an open meadow, or hear bull elk bugling in the fall. Two species of elk roam the state; Roosevelt elk in the west, Rocky Mountain elk in the east. The same is true for deer. There are two species; mule deer range from the crest of the Cascades east to the Idaho border and beyond, while black-tailed deer range from the Cascade crest west to the Pacific. Sometimes the two species interbreed where their ranges overlap.

Other large mammals include able-footed bighorn sheep, the elusive mountain lion, and North America's fastest land mammal, the pronghorn. With over 100 mammals found in Oregon, some of the smaller and more easily viewed include the porcupine, pika, and numerous squirrels.

Abundant in animal life, Oregon is also a virtual eden of botanical delights. In fact, the Kalmiopsis Wilderness is often called a "botanists paradise" and with good reason. About 1,000 plant species live here, including the rare Kalmiopsis leachiana. A pre-ice age shrub, the rose-like flowers bloom in May or June along Johnson Butte (Hike 5).

The oldest surviving member of the heath family, the wilderness was named for this unique flower found almost exclusively within wilderness boundaries. If you're atop Steens Mountain hiking the Desert Trail (Hike 23), you're bound to see an abundance of wildflowers if you plan your visit for early summer. Look for Cusick's buckwheat, a flower found no where else in the world.

One quick note. Many of the trails in this guide lead past meadows and ridges adorned with lovely wildflowers. Remember to see and smell the flowers, but please don't pick them. If you want a remembrance, take a picture, and leave the flowers for someone else to enjoy.

Oregon's trails pass through areas rich in botanical dreams, abundant animal life, lush forest, and dry desert. Some even provide wonderful views of the mighty Pacific. They are managed by the USDA Forest Service, Bureau of Land Management, Oregon State Parks Department, various counties, the John Day Fossil Beds National Monument, and Crater Lake National Park. More than half of the trails listed here rest in designated wilderness areas. The Forest Service manages most of these areas, although The Bureau of Land Management oversees several of these special areas as well.

What is wilderness? To some, it may mean a trip to the local park, to others it's a unique experience whereby one travels through the woods, enjoying peace and solitude. But wilderness as defined in this book is subject to those areas designated as such by Congress as a result of the Wilderness Act of 1964.

The first wilderness bill was introduced in 1956 by then Democratic senator Hubert Humphrey. John P. Saylor, a Republican House Member, and nine co-sponsors supported the Minnesota senator. The bill was finally passed in 1964 after nearly twenty hearings. President Lyndon Johnson signed the Wilderness Act into effect on September 3, 1964.

According to the law, wilderness "shall be administered for the use and enjoyment of the American people in such a manner as will leave them unimpaired for future use and enjoyment as wilderness, and so as to provide for the protection of these areas (and) the preservation of their character." If you're wondering what you can do to help keep the wilderness wild, be sure to read the chapter on ethics.

As you walk through the wilderness, imagine what it must have been like years ago when early inhabitants walked the land. They must have found a bountiful and fruitful land; certainly one of extreme beauty. Oregon's first inhabitants were thought to have arrived at least 13,000 years ago. Charcoal samples—collected from the Fork Rock Cave in northern Lake County—were age tested and determined to be from fires built at least 13,600 years ago. Other findings included a large number (between seventy-five and one-hundred) of sagebrush bark sandals. Found beneath the pumice and charred as though from hot ash, experts estimate the sandals to be around 9,000 years old.

While hiking you may find ancient artifacts or you may discover various forms of Indian rock art drawn on rimrock, boulders, inside caves, etc. While petroglyphs are by far the most common type of rock art, pictographs are also found. Petroglyphs are etchings made into the surface of the rock; pictographs are paintings made on rock. Please remember, it is against the law to remove the artifacts or to deface them in any way.

While some of the trails you'll hike were first hiked by native Americans, explorers, miners, fur traders and trappers, developed other paths. In 1805-06, Meriweather Lewis and William Clark explored the region from along the Columbia River to the Pacific. At this time, both British and U.S. adventurers were lured to the area by the lucrative fur trade.

But the real influx of people to the region began in 1842 when the first immigrant train—headed by Elijah White and partially piloted by Thomas Fitzpatrick—arrived via what is known as the Oregon trail. The following year, the "great migration" began when nearly 900 men, women and children followed the rugged trail. The flow of immigrants steadily increased with 1,400 arriving in 1844, 3,000 in 1845. For more than twenty years, thousands of emigrants traveled the 2,000 miles from Independence, Missouri, to Oregon City, Oregon. It wasn't an easy trip. Death was common; hardships neverending. It's no wonder the trail is often known as the "longest graveyard."

With thousands of immigrants arriving every year, England was pressured into relinquishing her hold on the Oregon Territory in 1846. Thus, Oregon, Washington, Idaho and parts of Wyoming and Montana west of the Continental Divide were free to become states. Oregon was admitted to the union with its present boundaries on February 14, 1859.

Oregon is a land that many thought worth dying for. Hike it's trails and you'll see why.

MAP LEGEND

Interstate	(00)	Described Trail and Trailhead	
U.S. Highway	(00)	Alternate Trail	
State or Other Principal Road	(375)		
Forest Road	[0000]	Cross-Country Route	
Paved Road		River, Creek, Drainage	
Dirt Road		Falls or Rapids	
Power Line		Meadow or Swamp	
Bridge		Springs	
Pass or Saddle		Lakes	
Building	■	Dry Lakes	
Camp site	Δ	Glacier	
Ranger Station			
Wilderness Boundary		State Boundary	
Peak & Elevation	0000	Map Scale and Compass	

0   0.5   1
MILES
N

BACKCOUNTRY ETHICS

After hiking hundreds of miles throughout Oregon, I have good news and bad news to report. First, the good news. I have to say I believe most people are conscientious and do not mean the backcountry any harm upon entering it. In most areas, I've found little trash. Sometimes I've found none. This is how it should be.

Unfortunately, there is some bad news. I've visited some areas where man has scarred the land, chopping down young trees for firewood, using an innocent lakeside for a bathroom. Toilet paper and human waste litter the ground, in view of all who pass by.

Changes are desperately needed. With more and more people venturing out into the wilds, perhaps we are loving our wilderness to death, or in some cases, not loving it enough?

What can we do to make a difference? What can we do to ensure a pristine wilderness for generations to come?

First, when you hike the trail of your choice, obey the rules. If a permit is necessary, be sure to obtain one before entering the area. Although permits are not necessary in most wilderness areas at the current time, Permit registration systems have been intitiated in some areas. Please contact the managing agency listed with each hike for current information.

Also, pay close attention to the type of traffic allowed on each trail. Some trails are open to foot traffic only. Others allow mountain bikes. Still others may be closed to horse travel. Many of the trails in this guidebook rest in designated wilderness areas where travel is limited to primitive methods only. These include backpacking, day hiking, horseback riding (although so me specific trails are closed to horses), or packing in with your favorite animal such as a horse, mule, llama, or even a back packing dog. Mountain bikes, motorcycles, and other mechanical or motorized methods of travel are not allowed.

Although Sam, my Samoyed, joined me on many of my hikes and backpacking trips, I know there are those who oppose dogs on the trails. In fact, dogs are not permitted on some trails, but they are permitted on all those in this guidebook, except for the Mt. Howard Trail (you have to ride a tram to the trail), and Mt. Scott Trail in Crater Lake National Park.

I realize that dogs can be a problem at times, but it doesn't have to be that way. I've run into noisy, messy dogs myself , but I've also observed quiet, obedient dogs. And I've never seen a dog litter a trail with beer cans. Keep your leashed pet quiet, away from the water when defecating (dog waste should be buried), and under control so he or she won't be off chasing the wildlife, and you'll find your pet will add joy to every outing. Also, you may want to get your pooch a dog backpack. Dogs can carry their own food and supplies, allowing them to feel useful.

Next, be sure to stay on the trail. If it happens to be muddy, plow right through. Stepping off to the side, on higher, drier ground, only serves to create another trail. In some areas there are several trails parallel one to the other, sometimes three-abreast. As you hike along, be sure to hike single file as well. Trails several feet wide exist in some areas because some people insist on walking side by side.

Giardia Lamblia *can occur in any mountain stream.*

Other suggestions include using a camp stove for cooking. Some people love the warmth and comfort of a crackling campfire, but in some places that just doesn't work well. Use a portable camp stove unless there is ample firewood and no restrictions against building a fire. Even so, please use wood sparingly. If camped at an established camp, use an existing fire ring. If camped where no one has ever camped before, dig a hole in the dirt or sand, and build a small fire sans rocks. When the fire is out, douse with water and replace the dirt. Be sure all fires are dead out.

As far as litter goes, carry it out. All of it. Do not bury your trash because wild animals may dig it up. If you choose to burn your trash, remember, foil doesn't burn.

Many wonder what to do about human waste and women sometimes wonder what to do with their toilet paper after urinating. Use the "cat method" when nature calls. Dig down six inches or so (a lightweight garden trowel works fine), setting the top soil aside. After using your outdoor privy, replace the dirt and top soil, burying all matter, then stamp the soil and cover it with a few sticks or rocks if possible. When urinating, women can bury their toilet paper or bring along some Ziploc baggies for safe keeping until returning to civilization. Menstruating women can do the same—use Ziploc baggies—to carry out soiled sanitary pads and tampons.

If you're out backpacking, you'll need to find a place to camp each night. Meadows and lakesides may be appealing, but they just aren't appropriate for backcountry travel. Some managing agencies require that you camp more than 100 feet from any water source, including streams, springs, ponds and lakes. Other require a minimum of 200 feet from any water source. Check with the agency managing the area you plan to visit for more details.

Ridgetops provide excellent campsites. There's often a good view, and ridgetops are usually breezy, Mother Nature's incomparable system of bug control. If you want to camp near a lake, back off a ways, choosing a private site. You can walk to the lake for swimming or fishing.

On extended hikes, bathing becomes necessary. You may have to wash your clothes as well. Please engage in both activities away from the water. You can bath directly in the water, however, if you do so without using any soap. When brushing your teeth, or using soap for washing, stay at least 100 feet from the water and bury your toothpaste.

Those entering the wilderness via horseback, should note that there's a limit to the number of animal/person groups allowed in each party. Groups are usually restricted to ten or twelve. For example, if twelve is the limit, you're allowed ten people and two pack animals, or six people and six pack animals. Pack animals must be picketed at least 200 feet from any water source. You'll also have to carry feed.

In popular horse country, hikers and horseback riders will undoubtedly meet on the trails. Please note, horseback riders have the right of way. Hikers, if you meet a horse on the trail, move to the down side of the trail, and refrain from making any sudden movements or loud noises.

While many enter the backcountry with relaxation, sightseeing, and photography or wildlife watching on their minds, some enter with hunting and fishing a top priority. Those interested in the last two activities will want to check with the agency managing the area they're interested in visiting. Those agencies can provide up-to-date information on permits and the opening and closing dates for various game.

By now, most backcountry visitors have heard about *Giardia lamblia*, a parasite, known to cause "backpackers diarrhea," a dreadful disease that may not die kill you, but from what I've heard you'll wish you had. Symptoms include severe abdominal cramps, gas and bloating, loss of appetite, and acute diarrhea.

No matter how pure the water looks, never drink from any spring, stream, river or lake without treating the water first. You can't see *Giardia lamblia*. Water sources listed in this book are not for straight drinking, but are sources you can obtain for treating.

Fortunately, not all water is contaminated, but because you can't tell by looking it's better to be safe than sorry. There are several water purification methods. First, you can boil all water. Most experts claim a minimum of one minute at altitudes below 4,000 feet should suffice; adding several minutes of boiling time for higher altitudes. Others recommend boiling all water for ten minutes, regardless of the elevation, just to be safe.

Some find a water purifier more convenient, although you'll have to carry the purifier. This is the metohd I use. Of course, boiling water takes extra fuel and it leaves the hiker with scalding hot water. Not the best idea if you want to drink the water right away. For those times, you can use commercial water purification chemicals. This is a last resort, however, as the water often tastes funny. Actually, awful is more the word.

Enough about rules, the do's and don'ts of appropriate backcountry travel. Why not grab your pack and head for the trail? And begin each trip with the saying "Take only pictures; leave only footprints," in your mind. By doing so, you'll leave a lasting treasure for future generations.

May God bless you as you walk the trail He has laid before you.

About the Trails

It's not always easy to judge the difficulty of one trail over another. I may think a trail should be rated easy and someone else will call it moderate. The physical condition of each individual and even the weather plays a role in what's hard and what's not.

To the best of my ability, I've rated the seventy-five trails in this guide as easy, moderate, and difficult. Sometimes you might even see a rating of moderate to difficult, or easy to moderate. It's often hard to pinpoint, especially when a trail is short, maybe less than a mile in length, but very steep. Is it easy because it's short? Or, difficult because it's steep?

An easy trail is usually a shorter trail, with gentle up and down grades. It might even be nearly flat. Moderate trails are longer in length, but usually less than eight miles. Elevation gains are usually no more than 500 feet per mile. Trails rated difficult are usually eight or more miles and have some steep gains and descents. These are the thigh pounders and calf busters.

Whether you're into easy trails or you demand the more strenuous types, have a safe and rewarding hike.

HIKING WITH CHILDREN

During the past few years I've talked to couples who have shared their love of backpacking, remembering back to a time when they climbed a favorite peak, strolled along a favorite stream, enjoyed the peace and tranquility of an uncrowded wilderness lake. But then they had kids and the hiking ended, the couple offering, ""We use to backpack all the time and then we had kids and that ended that."

Today, I am meeting parents who say "backpacking is a family sport."

Parents needn't stop hiking when children come into the picture. If properly prepared, parents can bring the kids along for anything from a short stroll along the beach, to an extended hike in the Cascade Mountains. Although you'll find hiking with children different than hiking with adults, it isn't that difficult. Just be ready to bring extra clothing and supplies.

What kind of a hike can you expect with children along? You can plan on taking plenty of breaks, covering the miles at an easy pace. (How tough can that be?) As you know, kids see things differently than adults. Be prepared to hike at their speed, stopping often so the kids can eat, play in streams or snow (snow is their favorite), and observe animal life. For best results, think like your children. Keep them busy and happy. Don't demand a certain number of miles per day.

Before you set out on an extended hike, I recommend starting out with several day hikes. It's the best way to see how far Junior can walk before he demands a rest? How does baby enjoy riding in his carrier? (Most babies love it.) If the day hikes go well, some parents have a practice camp-out in the backyard before heading for the wilderness. Others head for the trailhead, choosing a spot only a mile or so away from the car.

Bringing baby along takes special precautions. Babies' respiratory systems can't adjust to major elevation changes until one year of age. And because most babies refuse to wear sunglasses, you can't take them through snow country, or onto high exposed ridges where sunburn is a threat.

Short trips are best for those with babies, as diapers and bottles (unless breast feeding, the easiest method) must be carried in and carried out.

Toddlers, two- to four-years-old, are often the hardest to travel with. They're too big to carry, but not quite big enough to carry themselves over long distances. Plan no more than four miles a day with children of this age. Less may be better. As far as packs go, if your child wants to wear a pack, by all means let him or her do so. A tiny pack holding a jacket or toy will suffice. Later in the day, you'll undoubtedly end up carrying the pack, but the precedent is established. Around the ages of nine through twelve they'll be able to carry all of their own gear, including a fair share of the food. A cheap lightweight backpack makes sense.

Older children walk fast, often wanting to go on ahead to explore, being the first to discover their new surroundings. Although you'll want to encourage this newfound freedom, persuade children to stick to the trail and tell them to wait for you at every fork, touching bases at each junction.

One noteworthy precaution: Children of all ages, but especially the youngest ones, will be unable to tolerate bugs which tend to eat tender skin alive. Avoid buggy areas and buggy seasons for best results.

Children see the outdoors from an entirely different perspective.

Hikes your children will most likely enjoy include: Redwood Nature Trail (Hike 2), High Desert Trail (Hike 23), Mt. Howard (Hike 39), Arch Rock (Hike 44), and Munson Falls (Hike 70). The Isherwood Lake Trail (Hike 12) would make a good first-time backpacking trip. Just over three miles in length, the trail is nearly level and ends at a beautiful wilderness lake.

HIKE 1 *GRASSY KNOB*

General description: A short round-trip day hike in the Grassy Knob Wilderness.
General location: Ten miles east of the Pacific Ocean, near Port Orford.
Maps: Port Orford 15-minute USGS quad.
Difficulty: Easy.
Length: About .5 mile one way.
Elevations: 2,192 to 2,342 feet.
Special attractions: Great view, historic area, old-growth forests of Port-Orford cedar, Douglas-fir, hemlock and western redcedar.
Water availability: None.
Best season: All year.
For more information: Powers Ranger District, Powers, OR 97466; (541) 439-3011.
Permit: None.
Finding the trailhead: Drive north of Port Orford on U.S. Highway 101. Three miles north of Port Orford, go east (right) on Grassy Knob Road (Curry County Road 196). When the pavement turns to gravel (after four miles), take Forest Road 5105 until it ends at eight miles.

The hike: Thickly forested, extremely steep and rugged, this 17,200-acre preserve sees little use as trails are nearly nonexistent. Protected primarily because of the valuable anadromous fishery, Grassy Knob was established as wilderness with the passage of the Oregon Wilderness Act of 1984.

At the barricade you'll see a sign for the Grassy Knob Trail. Walk the road until it begins to level off. When you reach the crest at .5 mile, head up the bank to the right. Although unmarked, the trail is cut into the bank and there shouldn't be a problem in finding it. Grassy Knob is less than 200 yards from this point.

From the summit, there's a wonderful 180-degree view. You'll see the mighty Pacific Ocean and portions of the wilderness as well. At one time, a manned lookout stood upon this site, one with historical significance. During World War II, a plane launched from a Japanese submarine was seen from the lookout. There are even reports that the Japanese aircraft was shot at from here. For more information, read Bert Webber's *Retaliation.*

HIKE 1 *GRASSY KNOB*

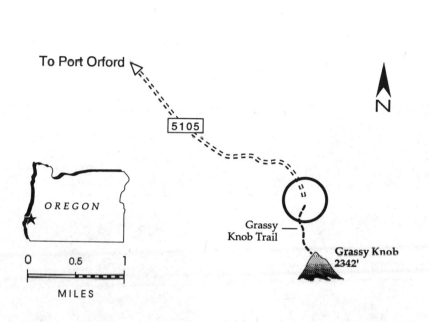

To Port Orford

5105

OREGON

0   0.5   1

MILES

N

Grassy Knob Trail

Grassy Knob 2342'

HIKE 2 *REDWOOD NATURE TRAIL*

General description: A short loop hike in the Siskiyou National Forest.
General location: Eight miles northeast of Brookings.
Maps: Mt. Emily 15-minute USGS quad.
Difficulty: Moderate.
Length: About one mile.
Elevations: 50 to 350 feet.
Special attractions: Wonderful stand of redwood trees, lush ferns, and many other plants and shrubs.
Water availability: Two small creeks.
Best season: All year.
For more information: Chetco Ranger District, 555 Fifth Street, Brookings, OR 97415; (541) 469-2196.
Permit: None.
Finding the trailhead: From Brookings, where you'll find all amenities, go south on U.S. Highway 101 for a short distance to North Bank Road which turns into Forest Road 1376 before reaching the trailhead. Make a left, following the sign to Alfred A. Loeb State Park. At 7.5 miles you'll pass the state park,

Hiker and Samoyed on Redwood Nature Trail.

located along the Chetco River, where there is camping (for a fee) and picnicking. Continue another .6 mile to the trailhead on the left.

The hike: Although there are some steeper sections along this trail, this hike is perfect for the entire family as it's only a mile in length and there are benches for resting and enjoying the forest.

At the trailhead, you'll find a pit toilet, picnic table, and informative brochures. You will find that numbered posts correspond to the brochure, informing one of the plants and trees found in the area. By reading the brochure you'll learn about redwoods, tanoak, Douglas-fir, rhododendrons, and much more.

Begin hiking Redwood Nature Trail 1111, following a small creek to a junction. Go left, hiking the trail in a clockwise direction.

HIKE 2 *REDWOOD NATURE TRAIL*

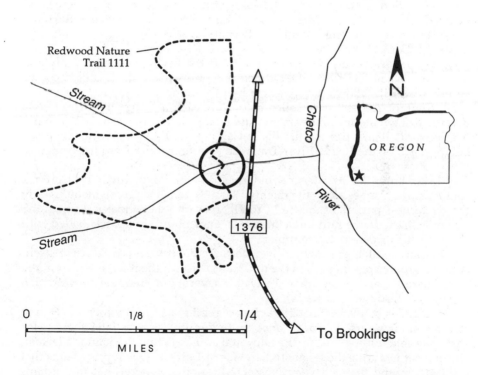

HIKE 3 *ROGUE RIVER*

General description: A two- to three-day round-trip backpack in the Wild Rogue Wilderness.

General location: About thirty-three miles northeast of Gold Beach.

Maps: Illahe 7.5-minute, Marial 7.5-minute USGS quads;Wild Rogue Wilderness map.

Difficulty: Moderate.

Length: About fifteen miles one-way.

Elevations: 207 to 425 feet.

Special attractions: Trail parallels famous Rogue River; great fishing, lovely streams, wildflowers, abundant wildlife—bear, deer, osprey, herons, and bald eagles.

Water availability: Numerous creeks cross the trail.

Best season: Usually accessible year-round, but spring and fall are best. It's cold and rainy in winter, hot in the summer.

For more information: Gold Beach Ranger District, 1225 South Ellensburg, Box 7, Gold Beach, OR 97444; (541) 247-6651.

For information on the various lodges along the Rogue River write to the Gold Beach Chamber of Commerce, 510 South Ellensburg , Gold Beach, OR 97444.

Permit: None required for hiking. Permits are necessary for rafting and kayaking. Contact the Forest Service.

Finding the trailhead: Reach the trailhead by driving east on County 595 from the coastal/river town of Gold Beach. County 595 (which later becomes Forest Road 33), follows the south bank of the famous Rogue River. Pass the small town of Agness three miles before crossing a bridge over the Rogue River, about twenty-nine miles from Gold Beach. Follow the right fork (County 375) towards Illahe, passing the Illahe Campground and the Foster Bar area before reaching the Rogue River Trailhead sign four miles from the bridge.

The hike: Enter the 36,000-acre wilderness via the Rogue River Trail 1160, a trail leading for miles along the mighty Rogue River. (This guide includes only the wilderness portion of the trail.) You'll cross into the wilderness about the two-mile mark. In the same area there is an enormous berry patch loaded with berries which ripen in mid-summer.

The trail parallels the Rogue River with frequent views of the river itself. Although there are times when the trail leads through the trees, away from the river, there are also times when the trail is several hundred feet above with a steep dropoff to the river below.

At 7.7 miles you'll reach Solitude Bar, a good place from which to observe rafters and kayakers. The area, once an Indian village, was later famous for early day gold mining. Just up the hill you'll come to Captain Tichnor's Defeat, site of a battle during the Rogue Indian War of 1855-56. One report claims that the Captain and his men were massacred; another reports that the Indians rolled large rocks down the mountain towards the white men, forcing them to retreat.

Reach Paradise Bar at 11.8 miles. It is a wild turkey management area, and dogs must remain leashed.

As you've probably noticed, this wilderness is different than most others.

16

Blossom Bar Creek

While motorboats and lodges are usually not tolerated, they are permitted here. When the Rogue River was designated wilderness in 1978 Congress demanded that the river continue to be managed under the Wild and Scenic River act of 1968, thus the boats and lodges.

On a special note, you'll want to watch for poison oak and wood ticks of which there are both.

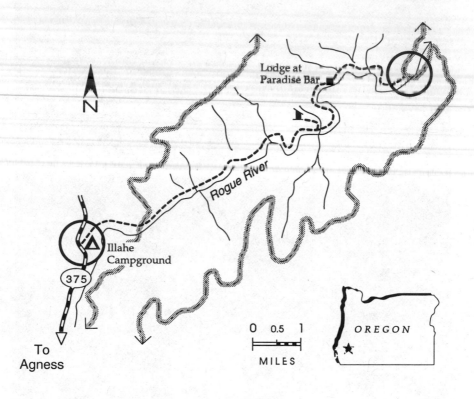

HIKE 4 *PINE FLAT*

General description: A round-trip day hike or a two-day backpack trip in the Kalmiopsis Wilderness.
General location: About twenty miles southwest of Grants Pass.
Maps: Pearsoll Peak 7.5-minute USGS quad; Kalmiopsis Wilderness map.
Difficulty: Moderate.
Length: Approximately 5.8 miles one way.
Elevations: 904 to 1,651 feet.
Special attractions: Wildflowers in the spring, fishing and swimming in the Illinois River.
Water availability: Numerous creeks exist along the trail although some are seasonal. The Illinois River provides water year-round.
Best season: Spring and fall are the best times; summers are very hot.
For more information: Illinois Valley Ranger District, 26468 Redwood Hwy., Cave Junction, OR 97523; (541) 592-2166.

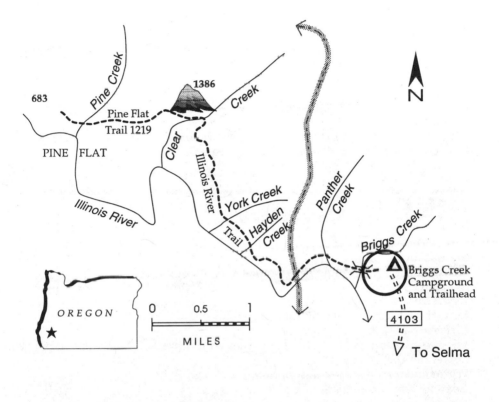

Permit: None.

Finding the trailhead: This hike begins at the Briggs Creek Trailhead. To reach the trailhead drive west on County Road 5070 (Illinois Valley Road) from Selma, Oregon, a small town off U.S. Highway 199. After 6.7 miles the road turns into Forest Road 4103; continue another 11.6 miles until the road ends at the Briggs Creek Campground. Please note, before reaching the campground the road changes from paved to well-maintained gravel, and then to gravel with limited maintenance. Although rough in spots, the road is usually passable with a passenger car. Cars with low clearance should avoid the road, however.

The hike: Originally designated a primitive area in 1946, the Kalmiopsis, Wilderness is one of Oregon's least-known and least-visited preserves. Many of those who enter the wilderness are botanists. With about 1,000 plant species (including poison oak), it's definitely a botanist's delight. It is also home to the rattlesnake and scorpion.

The hike begins via the Illinois River Trail 1162, with a bridge crossing over Briggs Creek. You'll enter the wilderness at one mile, hiking across a semi-open slope to the York Creek Botanical Area another mile down the trail.

You'll see the Illinois River as you climb and descend the slope to Clear Creek at 4.2 miles. According to the Forest Service, this creek lacks any siltation whatsoever. They claim that the water here is perhaps the clearest in the world.

Reach the junction of Pine Flat Trail 1219 at 5.1 miles. Go west (straight), descending the moderate to steep grade to Pine Flat. There are many nice places for camping in the trees with easy access to the river.

Those interested in fishing will find poor results in summer, but the fishing is fabulous in late fall when anglers hook steelhead, Coho salmon and fall chinook.

While exploring along the river, you might see remnants of an old trail leading to Weaver Ranch, an old, abandoned homestead, .3 mile from Pine Flat.

HIKE 5 *JOHNSON BUTTE*

General description: A round-trip day hike or two-day backpack trip in the Kalmiopsis Wilderness.

General location: About thirty miles east of Brookings.

Maps: Chetco Peak 7.5-minute USGS quad; Kalmiopsis Wilderness map.

Difficulty: Moderate.

Length: Approximately 7.5 miles one way.

Elevations: 3,200 to 3,920 feet.

Special attractions: Terrific views year round, rare Kalmiopsis leachiana flowers in the spring.

Water availability: See description.

Best season: Spring and fall; summers are very hot.

For more information: Chetco Ranger District, 555 Fifth St., Brookings, OR 97415; (541) 469-2196.

Permit: Registration box at the trailhead.

Finding the trailhead: Drive east on North Bank Road (County Road 784), located just south of the coastal town of Brookings, off U.S. Highway 101. After 10.6 miles the road changes to Forest Road 1376. Continue another 5.8 miles; turn right on Forest Road 1909 traveling another 9.6 miles to a fork. Keep to the left, reaching the signed trailhead in 5.5 miles.

The hike: Named for the rare Kalmiopsis leachiana, the Kalmiopsis Wilderness is a paradise for botanists and others interested in plants and flowers. This trail passes through several regions where the Kalmiopsis grows.

Begin hiking along an old mining road which is now Johnson Butte Trail 1110, keeping to the left when the trail forks shortly after entering the

Rhododendron flower.

wilderness. The trail climbs then descends, passing through the forest where rhododendrons blossom in the spring. At 1.4 miles look for a patch of Kalmiopsis leachiana on the east side of the trail.

Extremely rare, the pre-ice age shrub was first discovered near Gold Basin in 1930. Resembling a tiny, delicate wild rose (others think it looks like a miniature rhododendron), the patriarch of the heath family usually blooms in May or June. Except for a small patch in Oregon's Cascades and four sites just outside the wilderness boundary, it is found almost exclusively within the Kalmiopsis Wilderness.

You'll hike along a saddle at two miles and your reward for hiking this far will be a terrific view of your surroundings. As you continue across the open ridge, look for more Kalmiopsis and other wildflowers as well.

You'll come to a sign "water" at 5.2 miles. Salamander Lake is over the ridge, about 300 to 400 feet down a steep trail. Another sign pointing out a trail to water exists at 6.6 miles. A moderately steep spur trail leads to two small camp-sites, about 200 to 300 feet down the trail, and a year-round spring.

From here the trail climbs through a thick forest of trees and ferns then descends to a junction near Johnson Butte at 7.5 miles. Windy Camp and an unreliable spring is a short distance to the left.

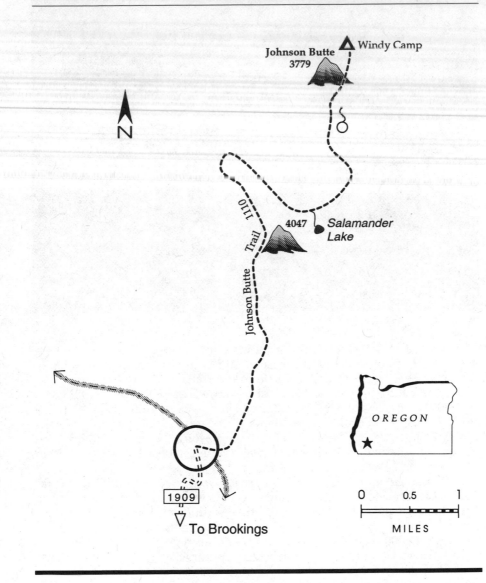

Johnson Butte
3779

△ Windy Camp

4047

Salamander
Lake

N

Johnson Butte Trail 1110

To Brookings

1909

OREGON

★

0   0.5   1

MILES

HIKE 6   VULCAN LAKE / LITTLE VULCAN LAKE

General description: A short day hike in the Kalmiopsis Wilderness.
General location: About thirty miles east of Brookings.
Maps: Chetco Peak 7.5-minute USGS quad; Kalmiopsis Wilderness map.
Difficulty: Easy.
Length: About 1.6 miles one way.
Elevations: 3,680 to 4,000 feet.
Special attractions: Good views, lake set in serpentine rock, California pitcher plants.
Water availability: Vulcan Lake, Little Vulcan Lake.
Best season: Spring and fall. Summers are very hot.
For more information: Chetco Ranger District, 555 Fifth St., Brookings, OR 97415; (541) 469-2196.
Permit: Registration box at the trailhead.
Finding the trailhead: Just south of the coastal town of Brookings, located off U.S. Highway 101, head east on North Bank Road (County Road 784) for 10.6 miles where the road changes to Forest Road 1376. Continue another 5.8 miles to Forest Road 1909; go right on Road 1909 to a fork 9.6 miles distant. Keep to the left, reaching the signed trailhead in 5.5 miles.

The hike: This trip is but a small sampling of the Kalmiopsis Wilderness, just north of the Oregon/California border. Referred to as a "botanist's paradise," the 179,862-acre preserve is home to the largest variety of plant species (about 1, 000 species) of any place in Oregon. In fact, botanists maintain that it nurtures more forest plant diversity than any other region of the United States except for the Smoky Mountains of the southeast.

Begin hiking an old mining road which is now Johnson Butte Trail 1110. Upon reaching a fork, a short distance from the trailhead, head right on Vulcan Lake Trail 1110A.

There are terrific views of the area as you climb then descend to Vulcan Lake. Along the way, see western azaleas and gnarled pines. Keep a sharp eye out for rattlesnakes.

You'll come to a fork in the trail at 1.3 miles, just before reaching Vulcan Lake. Turn right and go .1 mile to the lake. Little Vulcan Lake is nearby. Go back to the main trail, hiking 100 yards or so to another fork. Head right, descending to Little Vulcan Lake about .2 mile.

Look for the Darlingtonia, also known as California pitcher plants near Little Vulcan Lake. These plants are very unusual—they actually trap and digest insects.

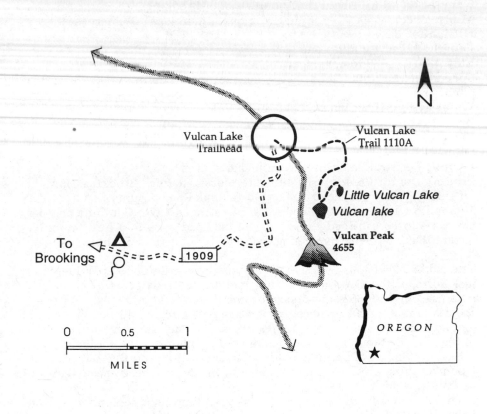

Vulcan Lake
Trailhead

Vulcan Lake
Trail 1110A

Little Vulcan Lake
Vulcan lake

Vulcan Peak
4655

To
Brookings

1909

N

0   0.5   1

MILES

OREGON

Trail worker and his donkey at Sucker Creek Gap.

HIKE 7 *SUCKER CREEK SHELTER*

General description: A day hike or backpack trip in the Red Buttes Wilderness.

General location: Twenty-five miles south of Applegate.

Maps: Grayback Mountain 7.5-minute USGS quad; Red Buttes Wilderness map.

Difficulty: Moderate.

Length: About 2.8 miles one way.

Elevations: 4,400 to 5,200 feet.

Special attractions: Wildflowers, deer.

Water availability: Sucker Creek and spring near shelter.

Best season: July through late October.

For more information: Applegate Ranger District, 6941 Upper Applegate Road, Jacksonville, OR 97530; (541) 899-1812.

Permit: None.

Finding the trailhead: Drive to the small town of Applegate located off Oregon 238, and head south on Forest Road 10 for fifteen miles. Turn right on Forest Road 1030 and continue another eleven miles until the road ends at the Steve Fork Trailhead.

The hike: Sucker Creek shelter is located in the Red Buttes Wilderness, a preserve comprised of rugged mountain slopes, those "you can see forever" sort of views, and multicolored meadows. Near the crest of the craggy Siskiyou Mountains, the wilderness straddles the California/Oregon border with most of the 20,234-acre preserve resting in California. The following trail and shelter, however, is in Oregon.

Begin hiking gradually up an old dirt road which now serves as a trail, and enter the wilderness. At .8 mile there's a not-too-obvious fork in the trail. Go right on Sucker Creek Gap Trail 906, climbing moderately though the trees. Along the way look for the long drooping branches typical of Brewer spruce.

At 2.8 miles you'll reach a junction. One trail heads to the right, two to the west. Of the two going west, the one on the right leads to Sucker Creek shelter. Follow the trail for several hundred yards until you see the shelter down the hill and to the right.

Originally used by cattle riders, the shelter was supposedly built in the late

1920s or early 1930s by Ashley Fulk, a rancher. Near the shelter, you'll find a trough filled with spring-fed water. This spot is a delight for wildflower enthusiasts and wildlife watchers as deer often feed in the flower-filled meadow surrounding the shelter.

HIKE 8 HUMBUG MOUNTAIN

General description: A round-trip day hike at Humbug Mountain State Park.
General location: Approximately six miles south of Port Orford, twenty-one miles north of Gold Beach.
Maps: Port Orford 15-minute USGS quad.
Difficulty: Moderate.
Length: About three miles one way.
Elevations: 30 to 1,761 feet.
Special attractions: Grand view to the south, lush forest, rhododendron display in the spring.
Water availability: Humbug Mountain State Park; both the campground and picnic area have piped water.
Best season: Year-round.
For more information: Oregon State Parks and Recreation Division, 525 Trade St. S.E., Salem, OR 97310; (503) 378-6305.
Permit: None.
Finding the trailhead: The trailhead is located off U.S. Highway 101 on the south side of the road, about six miles south of Port Orford where you'll find all services. If you'd like to camp (for a fee) at Humbug Mountain State Park, you'll find a short trail leading from the campground, under the highway, to the trailhead. The campground boasts hot showers, laundry, flush toilets, picnic tables, fire pits, and easy beach access. If picnic facilities are more to your liking, they are less than a mile south. Facilities include restrooms and picnic tables.

The hike: Although this trail sees a bit of use, it's a nice hike through lush forest, climbing up to the 1,761-foot mark for a grand view south to Cape Sebastian.

Begin hiking Humbug Mountain Trail (open to foot traffic only) which leads up through the forest at a moderate to steep clip for more than a .5 mile before easing up somewhat. Afterwards the trail climbs moderately past rhododendrons whose lovely pink blossoms decorate the trail in May and June.

As you climb, there are occasional views to the north and east, but you won't see a lot as dense forest obscures the view. No matter, reach the summit and a good view south at three miles.

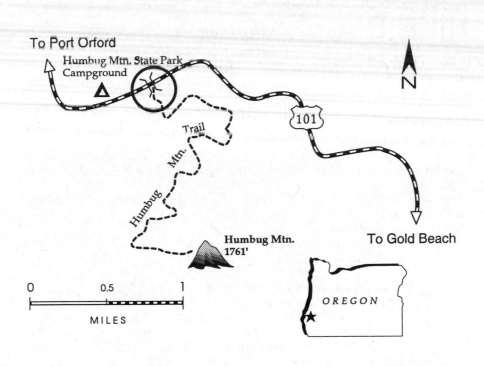

To Port Orford

Humbug Mtn. State Park
Campground

Humbug Mtn. Trail

101

Humbug Mtn.
1761'

To Gold Beach

N

0   0.5   1

MILES

OREGON

HIKE 9 NATIONAL CREEK FALLS

General description: A short day hike in the Rogue River National Forest.
General location: About sixty-seven miles northeast of Medford and seventy-nine miles northwest of Klamath Falls.
Maps: Recreation Opportunity Guide, available from the Rogue River National Forest.
Difficulty: Easy.
Length: About .4 mile one way.
Elevations: 4,000 to 3,760 feet.
Special attractions: A great family hike to a lovely waterfall; a wonderfully cool spot on a hot day.
Water availability: National Creek.
Best season: June through October.
For more information: Prospect Ranger District, Prospect, OR. 97536; (541) 560-3623.

HIKE 9 NATIONAL CREEK FALLS

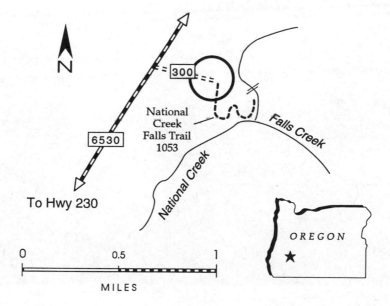

National Creek Falls.

Permit: None, although there is a registration box near the trailhead.

Finding the trailhead: Reach National Falls by traveling to the junction of Oregon Highway 230 and Oregon Highway 62, located about one mile north of Union Creek Resort. The resort offers a small market, cafe, and lodging. Campers will find the Farewell Bend Campground (a fee area) .4 mile south of the junction.

From the junction go north on Oregon 230 for 6.1 miles; make a right on paved Forest Road 6530. Travel another 3.6 miles to Forest Road 300 and make a right driving the gravel road to its end in .2 mile

The hike: This is one hike where you'll want to stuff a sack lunch in your day pack and drop down along National Creek for a picnic. Mist from the thundering falls is bound to keep you cool so plan the trip for a hot day!

Open to hikers only, descend the easy to moderate grade via National Creek Falls Trail 1053 for .4 mile. Along the way you'll hike under a dense canopy of mixed conifer forest. Don't worry about finding the falls dry—according to the Forest Service the creek flows year-round even in drought years.

HIKE 10 *MINNEHAHA TRAIL*

General description: A moderate day hike in the Rogue River National Forest.

General location: Approximately sixty-nine miles northeast of Medford.

Maps: Recreation Opportunity Guide (available from the Rogue River National Forest); Crater Lake National Park and vicinity 7.5-minute USGS quad.

Difficulty: Easy.

Length: About 3.1 miles one way.

Elevations: 3,825 to 4,400 feet.

Special attractions: Meadows, small waterfalls, solitude.

Water availability: See description.

Best season: June through October.

For more information: Prospect Ranger District, Prospect, OR. 97536; (541) 560-3623.

Permit: None.

Finding the trailhead: From the junction of Oregon Highway 230 and Oregon Highway 62 (about one mile north of Union Creek Resort where you'll find a small market, cafe, and lodging), go north on Oregon 230 for about 12.5 miles to Forest Road 6 530. Make a right on Forest Road 6530, a well-maintained gravel road, and drive one mile to Forest Road 800 where you'll make another right. Along the way you'll pass the entrance to Hamaker Campground (fee area) located about .5 mile down Forest Road 900 . Back on Forest Road 800, travel less than .1 mile to the trail. There's room to park on the right, just ahead. Please note, you'll pass a Forest Road 6530 junction after traveling about 6.1 miles up Oregon 230. Do not turn here!

The hike: Begin hiking Minnehaha Trail 1039, traveling through the trees on an old road. At .5 mile the road narrows to a standard trail as you begin hiking the Minnehaha drainage.

Although trail traffic is light today, this area was once popular with travelers walking or riding the old John Day Trail which passed just north of here at

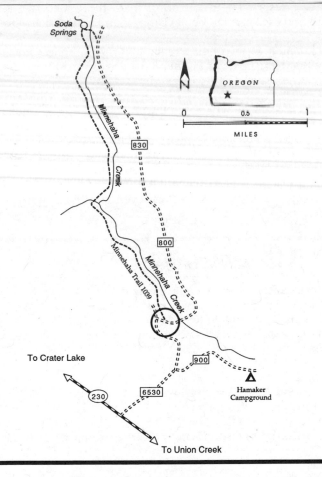

Lake West. Earlier in this century (1910), this wagon road became known as the Diamond Lake Road. Prior to this, the region was popular with miners and stockmen. The route was blazed out in the early 1860's, and was used for travel between John Day Valley and the Rogue River. Why the long commute? Miners dreamed of gold in the John Day Valley.

As you travel along through a potpourri of old-growth forest delights— Douglas-fir, western white pine, and lodgepole pine—look for deer and other animal life. Plant life includes wild strawberries, huckleberries (dwarf huckleberry lines some of the trail), and vanilla leaf.

The trail doesn't follow Minnehaha Creek for its entirety, but you will see the creek now and again and the trail crosses over the creek via a bridge near Soda Springs. Reach the springs at 2.9 miles and the trailhead at Soda Springs Trail 1039A at 3.1 miles.

Those wishing to hike one-way can have a shuttle waiting at Soda Springs if desired. To reach this trailhead, continue past the trailhead on Forest Road 800 to Forest Road 830. An unmaintained dirt road leads here.

HIKE 11 ASPEN BUTTE / LAKE HARRIETTE

General description: A two-day loop hike in the Mountain Lakes Wilderness.

General location: Fifteen airline miles northwest of Klamath Falls.

Maps: Aspen Lake 7.5-minute, Lake of the Woods South 7.5-minute USGS quads; Mountain Lakes Wilderness map

Difficulty: Moderate to difficult.

Length: Just over sixteen miles.

Elevations: 5,720 to 8,208 feet.

Special attractions: Wildlife, including bald eagles and osprey, solitude, great views.

Water availability: Clover Creek, several lakes.

Best season: Mid-June through late October. This area is also popular with snowshoe buffs and cross-country skiers in the winter.

For more information: Klamath Ranger District, 1936 California Ave., Klamath Falls, OR 97601; (541) 885-3400.

Permit: None.

Finding the trailhead: Drive to the triple junction of U.S. Highway 97, Oregon 140 and Oregon 66, near Klamath Falls. Head southwest on Oregon 66 for nine miles to Keno. Turn right on Clover Creek Road (County Road 603) and continue to a junction at nineteen miles; go northeast on Forest Road 3852 for 3.5 miles to the trailhead.

The hike: Several trails lead to the Mountain Lakes Loop Trail which in turn leads to Aspen Butte and Lake Harriette. This guide begins in the south end of the preserve at the Clover Creek Trailhead.

Enter the 23,071-acre wilderness via Clover Creek Trail 3722, a path that parallels Clover Creek beginning at the .7-mile mark. Embraced by lush ferns and colorful wildflowers, the creek is a delight to hike beside.

The trail climbs moderately along the creek, reaching the Mountain Lakes Loop Trail 3727 after two miles. Turn right here, climbing moderately through a forest of hemlock and fir, sometimes hiking near the edge of the old caldera rim.

Once a massive volcano reaching 12,000 feet into the heavens, the crown of the volcano collapsed forming a crater or caldera. Eventually snow and ice accumulated, glaciers formed, the contents dribbling over the rim and slowly down the sides of the mountain. Wind, water, and repeated glaciation reformed the mountain, leaving what you see today—fragments of the rim and portions of the base.

You'll reach the junction to Aspen Butte at about four miles. Head south up the unmaintained trail, climbing the moderate to steep slope past stunted firs and pines. Although portions of the trail are unmarked, the summit is easy to find. After again of 688 feet and just over a mile, you'll see 360 degrees to Upper Klamath Lake, the second largest body of water in Oregon, Mt. McLoughlin, southern Oregon's highest peak, and California's Mt. Shasta.

Continue to Lake Harriette by going back to the junction and descending via the Mountain Lakes Loop Trail, reaching the north shore of the lake at about six miles. The largest and deepest lake in the wilderness, seventy-acre

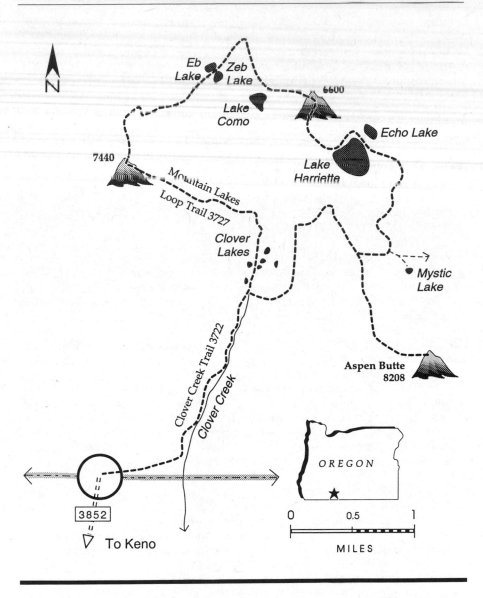

Lake Harriette is stocked with rainbow trout and brook trout.

Although you can reach the trailhead by going back the same way you came in, you might want to consider staying on the Mountain Lakes Trail, hiking counter-clockwise past several lakes, en route to the trailhead.

Lake Harriette.

HIKE 12 *ISHERWOOD LAKE*

General description: A round-trip day hike in the Sky Lakes Wilderness.
General location: About thirty-five miles northwest of Klamath Falls.
Maps: Pelican Butte 7.5-minute USGS quad; Sky Lakes Wilderness map.
Difficulty: Moderate.
Length: About 3.2 miles one way.
Elevations: 5,800 to 6,080 feet.
Special attractions: Trail leads past numerous lakes for swimming, fishing and camping.
Water availability: See description.
Best season: Late June though October. Also popular with cross-country skiers and snowshoers during winter.
For more information: Klamath Ranger District, 1936 California Avenue, Klamath Falls, OR 97601; (541) 885-3400.
Permit: None.
Finding the trailhead: Drive Oregon 140 to Forest Road 3651, about five miles east of Lake of the Woods. Head north on Forest Road 3651 for 10 miles to the trailhead at Cold Springs Camp.

The hike: Hike Cold Springs Trail 3710, crossing into the wilderness in .5

Mushrooms growing in the Sky Lakes Wilderness.

mile. Reach the South Rock Creek Trail junction a few hundred yards up the trail. Keep to the left, continuing on the Cold Springs Trail.

Isherwood Lake is but one of more than two hundred pockets of water in the Sky Lakes Wilderness. Blessed with an abundance of lakes and ponds, the 113,413-acre preserve attracts hordes of mosquitoes early in the season. Avoid the annoying insects by planning your trip for August or later.

At 2.4 miles you'll come to the junction of the Sky Lakes Trail. Head right on Sky Lakes Trail 3762, reaching the Isherwood Trail junction in another .3 mile; turn left on Isherwood Trail 3729.

Pass two lakes—Lake Natasha and Lake Elizabeth—on your way to Isherwood Lake at 3.2 miles. Popular with anglers, the lakes are stocked with brook,

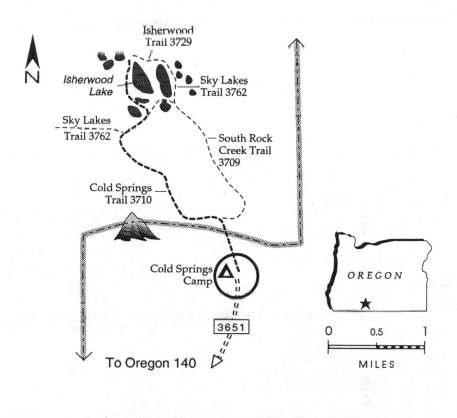

rainbow and cutthroat trout. Isherwood Lake is also an excellent lake for swimming.

In addition, wildlife watching is a popular pastime although mammals are often difficult to observe. Large game consist of Roosevelt elk and deer. Look for black-tailed deer on the west side of the Cascades, mule deer on the east. Near the crest the two species meet and breed. Other common mammals include black bear, coyote, chipmunk and porcupine.

If loop hikes are more your style and you don't mind adding less than a mile to your return trip, reach the trailhead by following the trail around the lake to SkyLakes Trail 3762 where you'll make a right. The trail leads past Heavenly Twin Lakes to the South Rock Creek Trail 3709. Follow this trail as it descends gradually to the trailhead.

HIKE 13 SKY LAKES LOOP

General description: A two- to three-day loop hike in the Sky Lakes Wilderness.

General location: Approximately thirty-five miles northwest of Klamath Falls.

Maps: Pelican Butte 7.5-minute, Devils Peak 7.5-minute USGS quads; Sky Lakes Wilderness map.

Difficulty: Moderate to difficult.

Length: About 25.5 miles.

Elevations: 5,800 to 7,582 feet.

Special attractions: Good views after a long hike through the trees.

Water availability: See description.

Best season: Late June through October.

For more information: Klamath Ranger District, 1936 California Avenue, Klamath Falls, OR 97601; (541) 885-3400.

Permit: None.

Finding the trailhead: Drive Oregon 140 to Forest Road 3651, about five miles east of Lake of the Woods. Go north on Forest Road 3651 for 10 miles to the trailhead at Cold Springs Camp.

The hike: Although ice fields and glaciers once covered this lake-blessed wilderness, present-day hikers see a different land, one without ice fields, without glaciers. They can and do, however, find remnants of the past to explore: Lakes fill glacial depressions and volcano cores beg for attention.

Hike the Cold Springs Trail 3710, crossing into the wilderness at .5 mile, reaching a fork .2 mile beyond. Take the left fork , staying on Trail 3710. The trail on the right will be your return trail.

After two miles reach the Sky Lakes Trail junction. Go left on the Sky Lakes Trail 3762, passing Deer Lake en route to the Pacific Crest Trail (PCT) at 3.8 miles; head north (right) on the PCT.

As you hike along the crest, you'll pass through forest then out across an open slope where you'll see Upper Klamath Lake, Oregon's largest natural lake. Back into the trees, you'll eventually hike in the open where good views are the norm. Reach the 7,300-foot saddle between Devils Peak and Lee Peak— the highest point on Oregon's section of the PCT— at 11.9 miles. A spur trail leads from the summit to the top of 7,582-foot Devils Peak for a 360 degree view of the surrounding wilderness and points beyond.

For the return hike, head back down (south) on the PCT to Snow Lakes Trail 3739 where you'll make a left, descending to the first of many upcoming lakes at 14.7 miles. You'll reach Martin Lake in less than three miles.

Snow Lakes is next in line with Luther Mountain painting a beautiful backdrop. The lake, which is good for swimming, is stocked with brook trout as are many of the area lakes. Continue south to Margurette Lake and Trappers Lake.

At Trappers Lake you'll begin hiking the Sky Lakes Trail 3762, going south past Lake Sonya to the Isherwood Trail junction at twenty-one miles. Turn right on Isherwood Trail 3729, hiking past Isherwood Lake and Lakes Natasha and Elizabeth before reaching another Isherwood/Sky Lakes Trail junction at

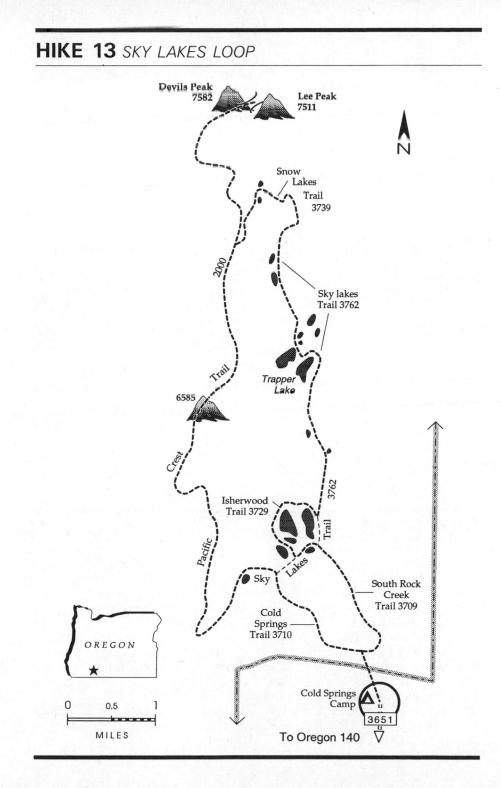

Devils Peak
7582

Lee Peak
7511

N

Snow
Lakes
Trail
3739

2000

Sky lakes
Trail 3762

Trail

*Trapper
Lake*

6585

3762

Crest

Isherwood
Trail 3729

Trail

Pacific

Lakes

Sky

South Rock
Creek
Trail 3709

Cold
Springs
Trail 3710

OREGON

0   0.5   1

MILES

Cold Springs
Camp

3651

To Oregon 140

Hiking in the Devil's Peak area.

22.5 miles. Make a left onto Sky Lakes Trail 3762, hiking past the smallest of the Heavenly Twin Lakes before reaching South Rock Trail in .5 mile. Turn right (south), hiking South Rock Creek Trail 3709 to the Cold Springs Trail and then on to the trailhead.

HIKE 14 *ALTA LAKE*

General description: A long round-trip day hike or a two-day backpack in the Sky Lakes Wilderness.
General location: About fifty miles northwest of Klamath Falls.
Maps: Devils Peak 7.5-minute USGS quad; Sky Lakes Wilderness map.
Difficulty: Moderate.
Length: About eight miles one way.
Elevations: 5,600 to 6,800 feet.
Special attractions: Scenic wilderness lakes stocked with trout.
Water availability: See description.
Best season: Late June through October.
For more information: Butte Falls Ranger District, P.O. Box 227, Butte Falls, OR 97522; (541) 865-3581 or Klamath Ranger District, 1936 California Avenue, Klamath Falls, OR 97601; (541) 885-3400.
Permit: None.

Finding the trailhead: From Fort Klamath, located about forty miles north/northwest of Klamath Falls, go west four miles on Nicholson Road. Make a left on Forest Road 3300 for .2 mile then turn right on Forest Road 3334. The road ends at the Sevenmile trailhead, six miles from Nicholson Road.

The hike: Alta Lake is one of seven lakes in the Seven Lakes Basin, perhaps one of the most beautiful areas in the Sky Lakes Wilderness. Located in the heart of the twenty-seven-mile-long wilderness, it is best visited mid-week when crowds are few.

Sevenmile Trail 3703 enters the wilderness just past the parking area and intersects with the Pacific Crest Trail (PCT) in less than two miles. Hike the

HIKE 14 *ALTA LAKE*

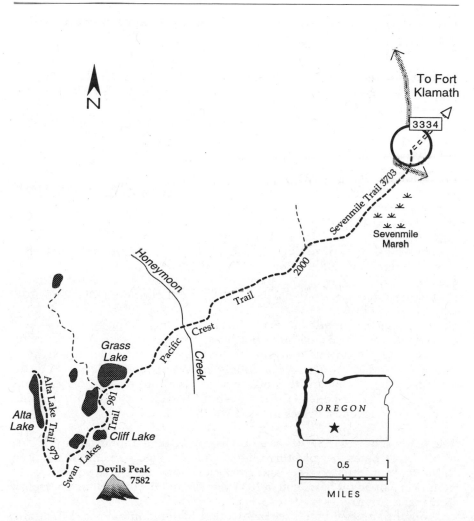

PCT, crossing Honeymoon Creek before reaching the Seven Lakes Trail at 4.4 miles. Turn right, hiking Seven Lakes Trail 981 past Grass Lake, Middle Lake, and on to Cliff Lake at 5.9 miles. (Lake Ivern Trail 994 passes between Grass and Middle Lakes en route to Lake Ivern and Boston Bluff for a delightful sidetrip.)

From Cliff Lake's north shore you'll see 7,582-foot Devils Peak. The north shore has been reforested so please use campsites on the south, east, and west sides of the lake.

You'll proceed by South Lake then climb moderately to the Alta Lake Trail junction at 7.1 miles. Turn right on Alta Lake Trail 979, hiking the level trail to Alta Lake at 7.5 miles. The north end of the lake is just over a half mile farther. From the ridge located on the east side of the north end of the lake, you'll see the Seven Lakes Basin and beyond.

HIKE 15 *MT. SCOTT*

General description: A round-trip day hike in Crater Lake National Park.
General location: About seventy miles north of Klamath Falls in Crater Lake National Park.
Maps: Crater Lake East 7.5-minute USGS quad; Crater Lake National Park Visitors map.
Difficulty: Moderate.
Length: About 2.5 miles one way.
Elevations: 7,700 to 8,929 feet.
Special attractions: The park's best overall view of Crater Lake and surrounding areas.
Water availability: None.
Best season: July through mid-October.
For more information: Superintendent, Crater Lake National Park, P.O. Box 7, Crater Lake, OR 97604; (541) 594-2811.
Permit: None for day hikes, however there is an entry fee at the entrance station to Crater Lake National Park. Pets are not permitted except on roadways and in vehicles.
Finding the trailhead: Mt. Scott Trailhead is located on the east side of Crater Lake, about sixteen miles northeast of the park's south entrance off Oregon 62. After driving four miles from the south entrance, turn right on thirty-three-mile Rim Drive, continuing another twelve miles or so to the trailhead. After hiking up Mt. Scott, be sure to continue the loop drive around Crater Lake. Perhaps one of the most beautiful in all of Oregon, it might just be one of the loveliest drives in all of North America.

The hike: A dirt road serves as a trail as you begin climbing along the base of Mt. Scott. Later the road turns into a wide path as you climb moderately to the summit. Stunted trees and great views reward you as you climb the mountain named for Levi Scott, a 1844 pioneer and the founder of Scottsburg, in Douglas County.

From the summit, you'll see many other high mountain peaks including Mt. McLoughlin, the Three Sisters, Mt. Jefferson, and California's own

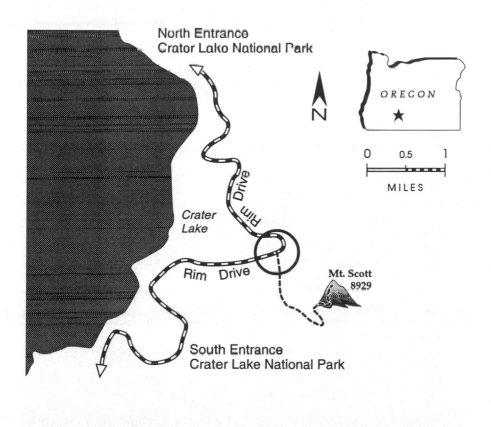

Mt. Shasta. Of course, you'll also see awe-inspiring Crater Lake (best viewed during the early morning hours).

Upon viewing the lake, it's impossible not to wonder how something so beautiful ever came to be. A half million years ago Mt. Mazama spewed forth massive amounts of magma, the mountain growing to an estimated 12,000 feet. After cooling, glaciers formed on Mazama's slopes, periodically masking the flanks of the immense cone and carving out the U-shaped valleys seen today. And then the climatic eruptions began.

About 6,800 years ago the mountain emptied from within, magma shooting towards the heavens. Mt. Mazama collapsed, leaving a vast bowl-shaped caldera in its place.

Today, Mt. Mazama lies scattered over eight states and three Canadian provinces. Researchers claim that ash (six inches deep) covered more than 5,000 square miles. Ash lies fifty feet deep in the Pumice Desert, located in the northern part of the preserve.

Water didn't fill in the crater right away. For one thing, the caldera floor was too hot, and volcanic processes hadn't ceased. Wizard Island (seen today) and Merriam Cone (hidden underwater)—both volcanoes in a volcano—were developing. Once volcanic activity subsided, however, the lake filled with rain and snow. The lake widened (it's nearly six miles wide) and deepened (it's 1,932 feet deep), making this the seventh deepest lake in the world.

HIKE 16 *ABBOTT BUTTE*

General description: A short day hike in the Rogue-Umpqua Divide Wilderness.
General location: Fifty-five miles northeast of Medford.
Maps: Abbott Butte 7.5-minute USGS quad; Rogue Umpqua Wilderness map.
Difficulty: Moderate.
Length: Approximately 2.5 miles one way.
Elevations: 5,200 to 6,131 feet.
Special attractions: Wonderful views.
Water availability: None.
Best season: Late June through November.
For more information: Tiller Ranger District, 27812 Tiller Trail Hwy., Tiller, OR 97484; (541) 825-3201.
Permit: None.
Finding the trailhead: Go to the junction of Oregon 62 and Forest Road 68, located four miles south of Union Creek. Turn west on Forest Road 68, continuing past the Abbott Creek Campground, en route to Forest Road 30 at 12.5 miles. Turn right onto Road 30, driving .5 mile to Forest Road 950; Abbott Butte Trailhead is .2 mile farther at the end of Road 950.

The hike: Hike Rogue-Umpqua Divide Trail 1470, an old dirt road leading to Windy Gap and the wilderness boundary at .7 mile. Continue another 1.3 miles to the junction of Abbott Butte. The half-mile climb affords a commanding view of the surrounding area.

This is the second such lookout atop the butte, built in the 1930s by the Civilian Conservation Corp. Although it was last used on a regular basis in the 1960s, it was considered an emergency lookout until the area was designated wilderness in 1984. Although some districts have chosen to remove structures such as this, the Tiller Ranger District has decided to leave the historic structure as it is and let it crumple through natural processes.

Special Note: Those interested in hiking farther down the Rogue-Umpqua Divide Trail may want to continue another 1.4 miles to two small ponds inhabited by beavers. Also, there's a commanding view of Elephant Head, a unique rock formation.

Abbott Butte Tower.

HIKE 16 *ABBOTT BUTTE*

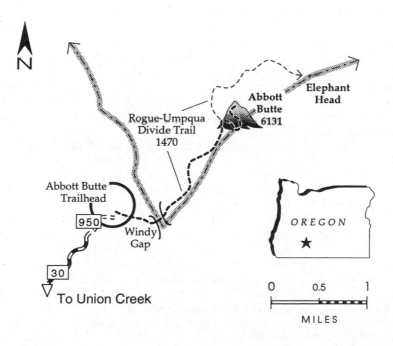

HIKE 17 *FISH LAKE / ROCKY RIDGE LOOP*

General description: A long, loop day hike or a two-day backpack in the Rogue-Umpqua Divide Wilderness.
General location: Sixty miles northeast of Medford.
Maps: Fish Mountain 7.5-minute, Buckeye Lake 7.5-minute USGS quads; Rogue-Umpqua Wilderness map.
Difficulty: Moderate.
Length: About 13.7 miles.
Elevations: 3,400 to 6,000 feet.
Special attractions: Endangered species such as the bald eagle and peregrine falcon, grand views.
Water availability: Highrock Creek, Fish Lake; none available on the second half of the hike.
Best season: Late June through October/November.
For more information: Tiller Ranger District, 27812 Tiller Trail Hwy., Tiller, OR 97484; (541) 825-3201 and/or Prospect Ranger District, Prospect, OR 97536; (541) 560-3623.
Permit: None.
Finding the trailhead: Drive Oregon 230 to Forest Road 6510, located two miles north of Union Creek. Head west (left) on Road 6510 and continue for 1.6 miles; take Forest Road 6520 for .4 mile; turn left on Forest Road 6515, driving 6.8 miles to Forest Road 530. Drive Road 530 1.6 miles to the Hershberger Mountain Trailhead.

The hike: The Rogue-Umpqua Divide Wilderness rests on the western side of the Cascade Range, in the old western Cascade range of mountains, a range developed millions of years before the present-day Cascades were formed.

Hike the Rogue-Umpqua Divide Trail 1470, climbing and descending to Fish Lake Trail 1570, one mile from the trailhead. Go left on Trail 1570, (the other trail will be your return), passing through Highrock Meadow then descending alongside Highrock Creek. Colorful deciduous trees reward those hiking in the fall.

You'll reach Fish Lake at approximately four miles. Here, anglers vie for rainbow, brook, and German brown trout. One note of interest: You'll undoubtedly notice a parasite growing on the sides of the brook trout. The Forest Service reports that the tiny, black, pinhead-size parasites do not harm the fish, nor will they hurt the humans who devour them.

Continue past Fish Lake, reaching Beaver Swamp Trail 1569 at just over five miles. Head right and up the trail to the Beaver Swamp Trailhead at 6.2 miles. There's a sign pointing the way to your destination, Rocky Rim Trail 1572.

Climb moderately through the forest, crossing in and out of the wilderness boundary, then out along an open slope where there are fabulous views of Fish Lake and much of the 33,200-acre wilderness.

In fact, the views are outstanding along much of the trail. Of particular interest is the rocky region known as the Palisades. Farther along, near the ten-mile mark, you'll cross a saddle—about five feet wide—with magnificent views of Diamond Peak, Mt. Bailey and Mt. Thielsen.

HIKE 17 *FISH LAKE/ROCKY RIDGE LOOP*

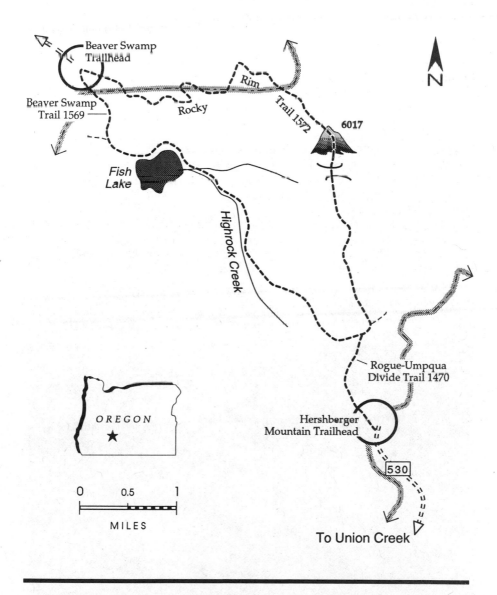

Beaver Swamp
Trailhead

Beaver Swamp
Trail 1569

Rocky

Rim

Trail 1572

6017

N

Fish
Lake

Highrock Creek

Rogue-Umpqua
Divide Trail 1470

OREGON

★

Hershberger
Mountain Trailhead

530

0   0.5   1

MILES

To Union Creek

Cross a couple of meadows as you continue, descending to the Rogue-Umpqua Divide Trail 1470 at 12.4 miles; go right, hiking Trail 1470 to the trailhead.

HIKE 18 *THIELSEN CREEK*

General description: A two- to three-day round-trip backpack in the Mt. Thielsen Wilderness.

General location: Seventy-seven miles southwest of Bend.

Maps: Miller Lake 7.5-minute, Mount Thielsen 7.5-minute USGS quads; Mt. Thielsen Wilderness map.

Difficulty: Moderate.

Length: About 11.7 miles.

Elevations: 5,640 to 7,560 feet.

Special attractions: Grand vistas, wildflowers, close-up views of Mt. Thielsen and Oregon's most southerly glacier.

Water availability: Evening Creek, Homer Springs, Thielsen Creek.

Best season: Early July through late September.

For more information: Chemult Ranger District, P.O. Box 150, Chemult, OR 97731; (541) 365-7001 or Diamond Lake Ranger District, HC 60/Box 101, Idleyld Park, OR 97447, (541) 498-2531.

Permit: None.

Finding the trailhead: The trail begins at Miller Lake, located about thirteen miles east of Chemult, a small town off U.S. Highway 97. Just north of Chemult, turn left on Forest Road 9772, driving past the Digit Campground to the day use area. The trail is near the shore.

Donna Ikenberry, Sam, and a friend with Tipsoo Peak in the background.

The hike: The Mt. Thielsen Wilderness is a potpourri of lovely mountain streams, a rushing river, lofty peaks, and a whole lot more. Located along the crest of the mighty Cascades, the 55,100-acre wilderness is but a small part of the larger Oregon Cascades Recreation Area.

Hike Miller Lake Trail 3725A through the trees, traveling along the northwest side of the lake. Along the way look for beavers who live and work here and at Evening Creek. Turn left at just over one mile, entering the wilderness and crossing Evening Creek. Gradually climb to the Pacific Crest Trail (PCT) junction at 2.7 miles.

Head left (south), hiking a series of slopes and switchbacks to rocky outcrops and wonderful views at five and just over six miles.

HIKE 18 *THIELSEN CREEK*

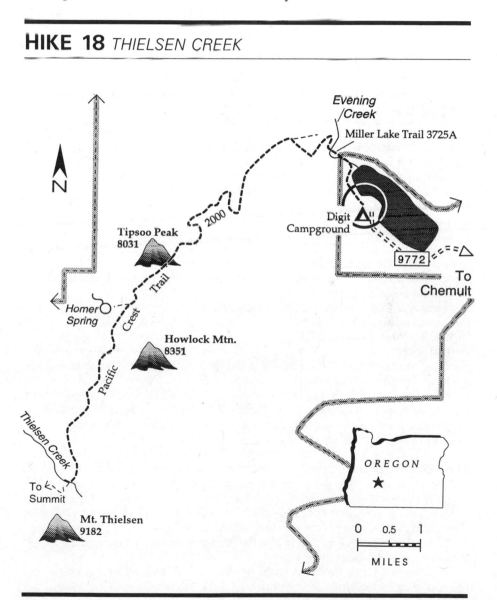

Farther along you'll hike across open slopes and meadows where there are terrific views of nearby Tipsoo Peak. You'll reach the junction of Homer Spring at eight miles. Look for the spring less then .5 mile west on Trail 1473.

Continue through trees and meadows, with views of Mt. Thielsen and nearby Mt. Bailey along the way. Reach the Thielsen Creek Trail 1449 junction at 11.7 miles. There are some flat areas for camping just down the trail.

Thielsen Creek is a few hundred yards ahead on the PCT. There's a sensational view of the area by hiking up the creek to the saddle at the northeast base of Mt. Thielsen.

Often called the "lightning rod of the Cascades," Mt. Thielsen's Matterhorn-like spire attracts countless lightning bolts. Those wishing to reach its summit should continue south on the PCT to a trail leading from the southeast side of the mountain to a point near the summit. Only those with mountaineering experience should consider the final scramble to the top.

HIKE 19 *BOULDER CREEK*

General description: A day hike (with shuttle access) or a two- to three-day round-trip backpack in the Boulder Creek Wilderness.
General location: Fifty miles east of Roseburg.
Maps: Illahee Rock 7.5-minute, Toketee Falls 7.5-minute USGS quads; Boulder Creek Wilderness map.
Difficulty: Moderate to difficult.
Length: About ten miles one way.
Elevations: 2,200 to 5,300 feet.
Special attractions: Solitude, old-growth forest.
Water availability: Boulder Creek, Onion Creek, Spring Creek, between the three- and six-mile marks.
Best season: Mid-June through early November.
For more information: Diamond Lake Ranger District, HC 60 Box 101, Idleyld Park, OR 97447; (541) 498-2531.
Permit: None.
Finding the trailhead: Reach the Bear Camp Trailhead, at the north end of the preserve, by driving to the junction of Oregon 138 and Forest Road 38, eighteen miles east of Idleyld Park. Go northeast on Forest Road 38 for eleven miles then turn right on Forest Road 3817. Drive three miles; head down Forest Road 3850 for eight miles. Road 3850 turns into Forest Road 3810 at this point; continue for 1.5 miles to the signed trailhead.

The hike: The Boulder Creek Trail stretches from one end of the Boulder Creek Wilderness to the other, the highest point being in the north, the lowest in the south. It's an ideal one-way trail for those with access to both ends of the trail.

Access to the southern trailhead—Soda Springs Trailhead—is via Oregon 138, about thirty miles east of Idleyld Park. At the sign Soda Spring Reservoir, head north then left on a dirt road, going past the dam and across the bridge to the signed trailhead, 1.3 miles from the highway.

From the Bear Camp trailhead, travel Boulder Creek Trail 1552, descending into the wilderness within a few hundred yards. Although you'll descend for

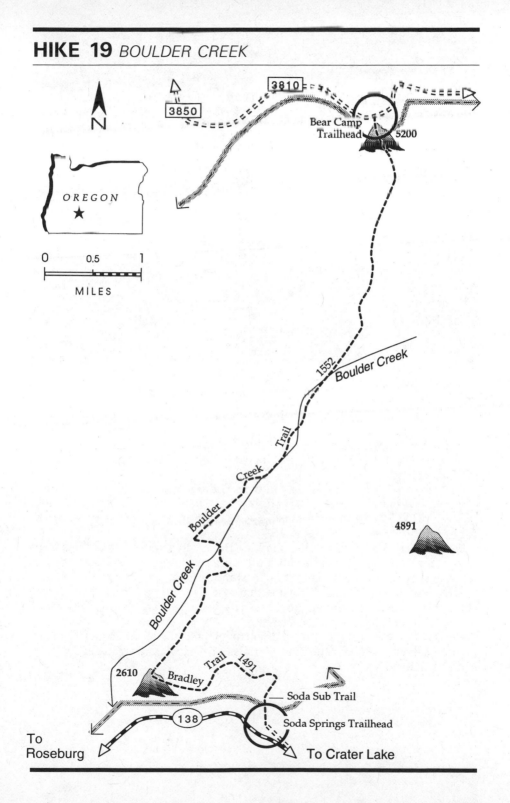

N

OREGON
★

0   0.5   1

MILES

3850   3810

Bear Camp
Trailhead   5200

1552   Boulder Creek

Boulder   Trail

Creek

4891

Boulder Creek

2610   Bradley   Trail   1491

Soda Sub Trail

138   Soda Springs Trailhead

To
Roseburg   To Crater Lake

Picking huckleberries in the wilderness.

the most part, you'll periodically climb as you make your way to Boulder Creek in about three miles.

A tributary of the North Umpqua River, Boulder Creek flows through the heart of the 19,100-acre wilderness, its waters an important spawning stream for anadromous fish.

Be sure to stick to the trail as you descend along the creek. Several other streams flow into the quiet pools and tiny waterfalls typical of Boulder Creek. You'll have to cross these streams as well as Boulder Creek every so often. All are easy fords.

From the creek you'll ascend to the Pine Bench area about seven miles from Bear Camp. Site of a 140-acre stand of Ponderosa pine, Pine Bench harbors what is thought to be the largest such stand this far north and west of the crest of the Cascade Mountains. Those interested in spires of basalt and unique cliffs should visit the Umpqua Rocks Geological Area, part of which is located in the southern portion of the preserve.

Head left onto Bradley Trail 1491 after traveling a little more than eight miles, then descend to the Soda Stub Trail 1.5 miles farther. Make a right and continue to the trailhead.

HIKE 20   *THE NOTCH*

General description: A long day hike or a round-trip backpack into the Gearhart Mountain Wilderness.

General location: About seventeen miles northeast of Bly; seventy-one miles north east of Klamath Falls.

Maps: Sandhill Crossing 7.5-minute, Lee Thomas Crossing 7.5-minute, Gearhart Mountain 7.5-minute, Campbell Reservoir 7.5-minute USGS quads; the Gearhart Mountain Wilderness Map.

Difficulty: Mostly moderate, but sometimes easy.

Length: Close to 6.3 miles one way.

Elevations: 5,920 to 8,300 feet.

Special attractions: Occasional breathtaking views, wildlife, wildflowers.

Water availability: An unnamed creek 2.4 miles up the trail and Dairy Creek.

Best season: Mid-June through early November.

For more information: Fremont National Forest, Bly Ranger District, Bly, OR 97622; (541) 353-2427.

Permit: None.

Finding the trailhead: To reach the Lookout Rock Trailhead, drive east on Oregon 140 from Bly—a small town off this main east-west Oregon artery—for one mile, then head north on Campbell Road. (Look for the sign "Gearhart Wilderness -17.") After about 0.5 mile make a right on Forest Road 34. Continue 14.4 miles to Corral Creek Road (Forest Road 012); follow the one-way dirt road 1.4 miles to the trailhead. You'll pass a campground and some horse corrals en route.

The hike: For those who are wondering, "The Notch" is the northern half of Gearhart Mountain. The top of the mountain is split in two, with the Notch estranged from the main peak for more than 300 feet.

There are several trails leading to the Notch, but this route is by far the most scenic. Soon after entering the wilderness via Gearhart Trail 100, you'll hike through the Palisades, rock formations born of massive porphyritic lava flows. Ponderosa pine are scattered throughout the rocky terrain. Farther along, you'll see the Dome, an imposing series of cliffs rising up to 400 feet above the surrounding terrain.

Along the trail there are fabulous views: Mt. Shasta, a California monolith stretching more than 14,000 feet into the heavens, is seen from a distance of more than 100 miles. From a saddle overlooking Dairy Creek, there are spectacular views of the 22,809-acre wilderness.

The trail descends from the saddle to Dairy Creek and your last dependable source of water. This creek will quench more than your thirst, however, as it winds through a wildflower-laden meadow with 8,364-foot Gearhart Mountain providing an impressive backdrop. Once past the meadow, there are favorable campsites.

You'll reach the highest point of the Gearhart Trail (8,040 feet) at about six miles. Hiking along the base of the mountain, you probably looked to the east and deemed a summit climb sans technical gear all but impossible. The crest, however, is easily reached by climbing the main south ridge.

On a clear day, views from Gearhart's highest point are awe-inspiring. Steens Mountain is visible to the east. To the west, a variety of Cascade Peaks stretch from California's Mt. Lassen to the Three Sisters in Oregon. Blue Lake is seen to the northeast. It is the only lake in the Gearhart Wilderness,

Backpacker and his Samoyed stand near "The Parallel," with Gearhart Mountain in the background.

and those with energy to spare can reach it by continuing to the north on the Gearhart Mountain Trail for four miles. Along the way you'll pass through a forest of toothpick-like lodgepole pine en route to the Gearhart Marsh, home for a herd of thirty to fifty Rocky Mountain elk.

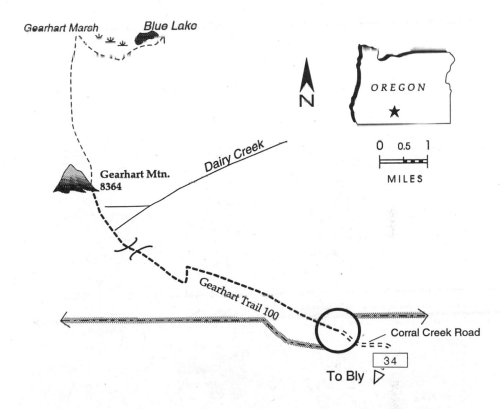

General description: A day hike in the Fremont National Forest.
General location: About twenty-two miles northwest of Lakeview.
Maps: Cougar Peak 7.5-minute USGS quad.
Difficulty: Moderate to difficult.
Length: About 2.9 miles one way.
Elevations: 6,200 to 7,919 feet.
Special attractions: Wonderful views, solitude.
Water availability: Trail follows Cougar Creek for the first mile or so.
Best season: Mid-June through early November.
For more information: Lakeview Ranger District, 524 North G Street, Lakeview, OR 97630; (541) 947-2151.
Permit: None.
Finding the trailhead: From Lakeview, where all services are available, go

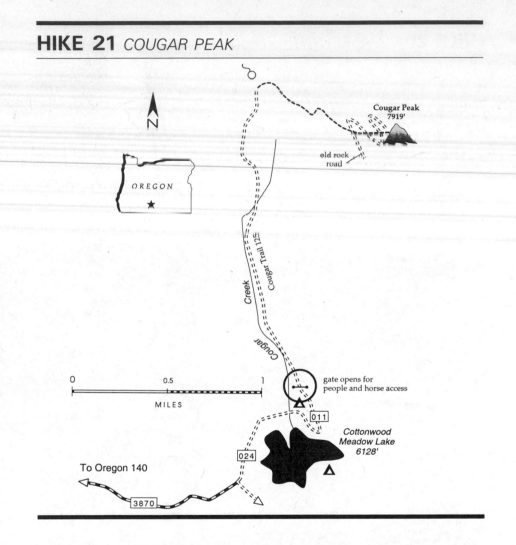

OREGON

Cougar Peak
7919'

old rock
road

N

Creek

Cougar Trail 125

Cougar

0   0.5   1

MILES

gate opens for
people and horse access

011

Cottonwood
Meadow Lake
6128'

024

To Oregon 140

3870

west on Oregon 140 for 22.6 miles; make a right on Forest Road 3870. A sign points the way to Cottonwood Meadow Lake. Drive the paved road to its end at 5.8 miles. Cottonwood Meadow Lake is just beyond with camping facilities on both sides of the lake.

To reach the trailhead and the Cougar Creek Campground, go to the left past the campground host on Forest Road 024, a well-maintained gravel road. Travel .7 mile to a picnic area/outhouses on the right, camping area on the left. If you are camping turn into the campground on Forest Road 011 and pick a spot. The trailhead is at the end of the road in .2 mile. If you are day hiking, park in the picnic area parking lot and walk to the trailhead.

The hike: This trail is perfect for those who'd like to set up camp at Cottonwood Meadow Lake, hiking to Cougar Peak sometime during the day. Cottonwood Meadow Lake is quite scenic. The small artificial lake, created in a joint effort by the U.S. Forest Service and the Oregon Department of Fish and

Wildlife in 1961, is stocked with both rainbow and brook trout.

Camping is free. Amenities include picnic tables, fire pits, outhouses, and water.

Begin hiking unsigned Cougar Peak Trail by traveling the old road past the campground. There's a gate, but the poles are easily removed to permit horses. As you hike along a pretty meadow lined with aspens, with Cougar Creek flowing through its heart, look for black bear, mule deer, coyote, grouse, and other wildlife.

Enter a clearcut area and Forest Road 013 at 1.4 miles. Cougar Peak is straight ahead to the east-northeast.

Continue straight on Forest Road 016 through the clearcut to a fork in about 200 feet. Go left, looking for the Cougar Peak Trail 120 (The Forest Service claims this is Trail 125, not 120) sign which you'll reach in another .1 mile. Proceed along the old road to another sign at 1.7 miles. Now climb at a steep grade; the road will turn into a standard trail along the way. The trail leads up through the trees, across some shale areas, and it crosses an old road on several occasions. Reach the summit and site of an old lookout at 2.9 miles. From the top you'll look down upon Cottonwood Meadow Lake and see many distant peaks, including California's Mt. Shasta.

HIKE 22 *CRANE MOUNTAIN*

General description: A short day hike in the Fremont National Forest.
General location: About ten miles southeast of Lakeview.
Maps: Crane Mountain 7.5-minute USGS quad.
Difficulty: Easy to moderate.
Length: About one mile one way.
Elevations: 8,240 to 8,456 feet.
Special attractions: Outstanding views, wildlife, wildflowers.
Water availability: None.
Best season: Mid-June through early November.
For more information: Lakeview Ranger District, 524 North G Street, Lakeview, OR 97630; (541) 947-2151.
Permit: None.
Finding the trailhead: From downtown Lakeview (where you'll find all services), go north on U.S. 395/Oregon 140 for 4 .7 miles. At this point Oregon 140 East branches off to the right. Follow it 7.1 miles to S. Warner Rd. (Forest Road 3915) an asphalt road which turns to gravel in a few miles. After traveling 10.1 miles on Forest Road 3915, turn right on Forest Road 4011 . In less than a mile you'll pass the turnoff (Forest Road 011) to the Willow Creek Campground. Free, you'll find picnic table s, fire pits, outhouses, and water.

After traveling a total of 3.6 miles on Forest Road 4011 the road changes to Forest Road 015, a narrow, rocky, dirt road. Those with low clearance vehicles will have to park here and walk to the trailhead in another 2.6 miles. En route to the trailhead, you'll see a dirt road taking off to the right. Follow this a short distance for a wonderful view from 7,515-foot Willow Point .

Before jumping out at the trailhead, you'll want to continue up the road another .2 mile to the site of an old lookout. From here there are terrific views of the Warner Mountains, the Steens Mountain, and beyond. You'll see into four states from here—Oregon, California, Idaho and Nevada.

The hike: Although Crane Mountain juts heavenward a mere ten miles from Lakeview, you'll have to drive around the mountain, doubling the distance before reaching the trailhead. The view from atop Crane Mountain is well worth the drive, however.

From at the trailhead, head south on the Crane Mountain National Recreation Trail—hiking nearly level ground for .8 mile. Once the trail begins descending start looking for orange flagging on the right. Flagging leads to the high point on Crane Mountain, approximately .2 mile to the west. Views are breathtaking from the ridge.

Those desiring a longer hike can continue along the Crane Mountain Trail which stretches a total of 8.7 miles from the site of the old lookout south into California. Along the way look for bighorn sheep, mule deer, coyotes, and other mammals.

HIKE 22 *CRANE MOUNTAIN*

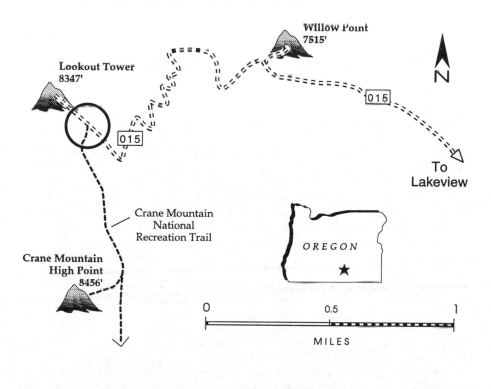

HIKE 23 *HIGH DESERT TRAIL*

General description: A short day hike to a wonderful close-up view of Big Indian Gorge, Steens Mountain.
General location: About eighty-six miles south of Burns.
Maps: Desert Trail Guide: Steens Mountain to the Alvord Desert.
Difficulty: Easy.
Length: About .5 mile.
Elevations: 9,000 to 9,090 feet.
Special attractions: Gorgeous views, wildlife, wildflowers.
Water availability: Spring.
Best season: July through mid-October.
For more information: Desert Trail Association, P.O. Box 589, Burns, OR. 97720.
Permit: None.
Finding the trailhead: To reach this segment of what is currently called the Oregon High Desert Trail, drive south from Burns (where you'll find all services), to Frenchglen, a small hamlet about sixty miles south on Oregon 205. There's a combination general store/post office here, a school, and the historic Frenchglen Hotel. Reservations are usually a must; dinner reservations are required. If you'd like to eat breakfast, lunch, or a small dinner at the hotel, you needn't be a guest there.

From Frenchglen, go east on Steens Mountain Loop Road, a gravel road, passing Camper Corral (Steens Mountain Resort) in three miles. Those interested in camping will find full hookups here; also there's a laundromat and showers. Those with more primitive camping in mind can continue another .1 mile to the turnoff for Page Springs Campground, a BLM facility resting on the banks of the Donnerund Blitzen River. For a small fee, you'll find water, pit toilets, picnic tables, and fire pits, about .3 mile off the main road.

The road is quite bumpy as you continue up the mountain. It is not recommended for trailers although I've seen them as far up as the Fish Lake Campground, 13.5 miles away. Passenger cars make the trip regularly, but a high clearance vehicle is recommended. Please note, the road is usually closed by snow until sometime in July.

From Fish Lake, where you'll find the same services as the Page Springs Campground, continue up the mountain passing another BLM Campground, Jackman Park, after driving 2.2 miles. Proceed an additional 3.9 miles to the turnoff for Kiger Gorge, a must-see. A magnificent viewpoint of the glacier-carved gorge is .4 mile farther.

From the Kiger Gorge turnoff, drive 2.8 miles to a junction leading to the East Rim and the Steens Summit, each more than 9,7 00 feet high. Both provide equally splendid views of the Alvord Desert, 5,000 feet below.

To reach the trailhead, continue from the junction, descending 1.1 miles to the signed Desert Hiking Trail on the left.

The hike: Perfect for those with children, or those who enjoy short day hikes, this portion of trail is but a small sampling of the larger Desert Trail, a proposed path that will eventually reach from Mexico to Canada.

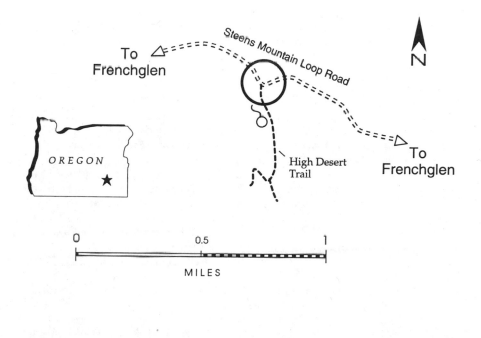

The Desert Trail Association, a conservation- and recreation-oriented organization committed to the development of the National Desert Scenic Trail, is pushing for such a trail. They also strive to protect the Western Desert.

Still in its infancy, no completion dates have been set for the trail, although several hundred miles of trail has been designated in Oregon, Nevada, and a small portion of trail exists in California. The nonprofit organization can use your help in making this 1,800- to 2,000-mile trail a reality. Contact them today for more information.

Follow an old jeep road which now serves as the trail and is closed to motor vehicles, passing a spring en route. Go .5 mile to a rocky outcrop and a view of Big Indian Gorge. There are several other closed roads in the area leading to equally good views.

To return to Frenchglen, you can continue driving the loop or head back the way you came. I'd suggest continuing the loop as it is a beautiful drive, reaching Oregon 205 in about twenty-nine miles. Frenchglen is another ten miles to the north via paved Oregon 205.

HIKE 24 DEAD HORSE RIM

General description: A short loop day hike in the Fremont National Forest.

General location: About twenty-six miles southwest of Paisley.

Maps: Lee Thomas Crossing 7.5-minute USGS quad.

Difficulty: Easy to moderate.

Length: About 3.8 miles.

Elevations: 7,372 to 8,134 feet.

Special attractions: Occasional views, wildlife, some wildflowers.

Water availability: None on the hike although there is water at the Dead Horse Lake Campground from which this trail originates.

Best season: June through early November.

For more information: Paisley Ranger District, Paisley, OR 97636; (541) 943-3114.

Permit: None.

Finding the trailhead: There are several routes into this region, but our trip began at the nearest town of Paisley, a small town offering a gas station/ market and cafe. Paisley rests on Oregon 31.

From the center of town, head west on County Road 28 which turns into Forest Road 33 soon after. Reach a fork in just under a mile; go right on Forest Road 3315, a well-maintained gravel road. Continue another 20.3 miles and make a left on Forest Road 28. After 2.7 miles make a right on Forest Road 033, a graded dirt road which leads past Campbell Lake and Campground at 1.8 miles and on to the Dead Horse Lake and Campground at 3.4 miles. The trailhead is .2 mile before reaching the Dead Horse Campground.

Both campgrounds are free and provide shady sites with picnic tables and fire pits. Water and outhouses are nearby.

The hike: From the trailhead, climb the moderate grade via Trail 140 past lodgepole pine and whitebark pine, among other species, to a good view of Dead Horse Lake at .4 mile. Lupine and paintbrush decorate some of the forest floor.

Reach a junction just past the view. Go right to continue to Deadhorse Rim. The fork to the left leads to Campbell Lake in 1. 5 miles.

Now it's an easy to moderate grade up to a junction at one mile. Go right again to continue the loop. Once more the left fork leads to Campbell Lake.

Come to a junction at two miles. Head right to continue the loop. For a good view of Dead Horse Lake and surrounding areas, continue to the left and up a short, steep grade. The trail levels off on top leading .3 mile to the junction of Dead Horse Rim Trail 139. Step off the trail and over to the ridge edge for several nice views.

Back on the main trail, descend moderately to a closed road at 3.1 miles. Go right another .2 mile and around a gate, now traveling a gravel road through the campground and back to the trailhead at 3.8 miles.

Special note: Hikers can begin hiking from Campbell Lake if desired. If so, add another 1.5 miles and 177 feet gain in elevation and descent to the loop.

HIKE 24 *DEAD HORSE RIM*

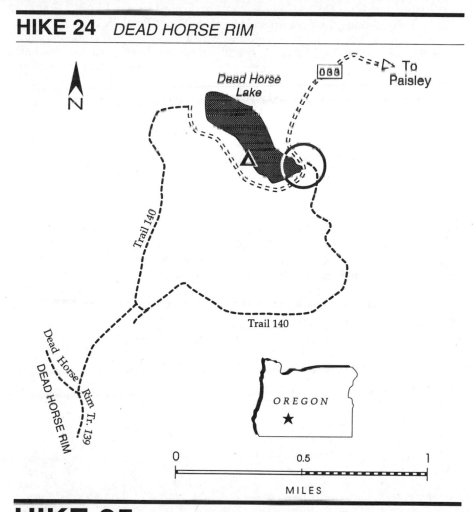

HIKE 25 *HAGER MOUNTAIN*

General description: A short day hike in the Fremont National Forest.
General location: About ten miles south of Silver Lake.
Maps: Hager Mountain 7.5-minute USGS quad.
Difficulty: Moderate to difficult.
Length: About 1.5 miles one way.
Elevations: 5,840 to 7,185 feet.
Special attractions: Grand views from the lookout. Wildflowers atop summit.
Water availability: Hager Spring is located at the trailhead.
Best season: June through early November.
For more information: Silver Lake Ranger District, Silver Lake, OR 97638;
(541) 576-2169.
Permit: None.
Finding the trailhead From the small town of Silver Lake, where you'll find

a gas station/market, cafe and motel, go south from Oregon 31 onto County Road 4-12. At 5.8 miles the paved road changes to Forest Road 28. After traveling nine miles from Silver Lake, turn left onto Forest Road 012, a dirt road (a sign points the way to the Hager Trail). Drive two miles to Hager Spring which has piped water. There are several camping areas nearby. Free camping is also available at nearby Thompson Reservoir, located about four miles to the south via Forest Road 28. Here you'll find picnic tables, outhouses, fire pits, and water.

The hike: Hike the moderate to steep trail through a forest of ponderosa pines and hemlock, emerging into the open near the summit. The crest is blanketed with rocks, wildflowers (in the proper season), and a fire lookout which you'll reach at 1.5 miles.

The lookout is manned from mid-June through mid-October. There's an outhouse near the summit.

From the lookout there's a wonderful 360-degree view. You'll see south to California's Mt. Shasta, 125 miles away. To the north see Mt. Jefferson, about 123 miles as the eagle flies. You'll see many other Cascade peaks including the Three Sisters, Mt. Thielsen, and Diamond Peak. Nearby highlights include Christmas Valley and many other high desert areas.

HIKE 25 *HAGER MOUNTAIN*

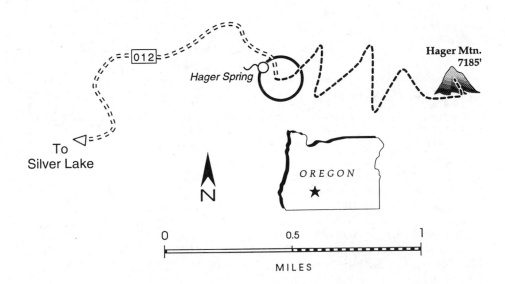

HIKE 26 *STEINS PILLAR*

General description: A short day hike in the Ochoco National Forest.
General location: About sixteen miles northeast of Prineville.
Maps: Ochoco Reservoir 15-minute USGS quad.
Difficulty: Moderate.
Length: About 1.8 miles one way.
Elevations: 4,400 to 4,700 feet.
Special attractions: Excellent view of the popular rock formation Steins Pillar.
Water availability: None.
Best season: April through November.
For more information: Ochoco National Forest, P.O. Box 490, Prineville, OR 97754; (541) 447-6247.
Permit: None.
Finding the trailhead: From Prineville, where you'll find all services, head east on U.S. 26, passing Ochoco Lake State Park en route. You'll find picnic

HIKE 26 *STEINS PILLAR*

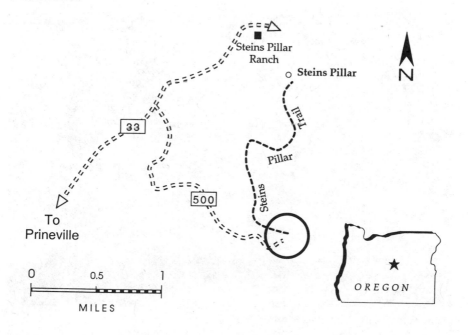

Steins Pillar/Steins Pillar Ranch.

and camping facilities (for a fee) here. At 9.3 miles make a left on paved Mill Creek Road which turns to gravel and Forest Road 33 in about five miles. After traveling 6.7 miles from U.S. 26, make a right on Forest Road 500. Reach the unmarked trailhead and a free picnic/camping area in 2.1 miles. There are picnic tables, fire pits, shady ponderosa pines.

The hike: Steins Pillar, a geologic wonder, rises more than 300 feet above the surrounding countryside. Although a good view of the pillar is an easy feat from the road, you'll want to hike this trail for a close-up view.

The trail starts from the camping area and leads through the trees then across semi-open slopes where juniper trees appear to be the norm. Some wildflowers grace the slopes early in the summer.

The trail is a moderate climb (some sections are easier, some steeper) to one mile then a descent of the same gradient to 1.8 miles and a terrific view of Steins Pillar.

Look for turkey vultures soaring above the pillar. You'll see down to the valley below, a drop of some 300 feet.

For a road-side view of Steins Pillar, head back to Forest Road 33; make a right and go another .8 mile. You'll see Steins Pillar and Steins Pillar Ranch from this point.

HIKE 27 *INDIAN CREEK BUTTE*

General description: A two- to three-day round-trip backpack in the Strawberry Mountain Wilderness.
General location: Seventeen miles southeast of John Day.
Maps: Canyon Mountain 7.5-minute, Pine Creek Mountain 7.5-minute USGS quads; Strawberry Mountain Wilderness map.
Difficulty: Moderate to difficult.
Length: About 9.6 miles one way.
Elevations: 4,800 to 7,760 feet.
Special attractions: Enormous ponderosa pines, great views, wildflowers, wildlife, and solitude except during the fall hunting season.
Water availability: Canyon Creek and other small creeks.
Best season: July through November.
For more information: Prairie City Ranger District, P.O. Box 337, Prairie City, OR 97869; (541) 820-3311.
Permit: Registration box at the trailhead.
Finding the trailhead: The trail begins at the East Fork Canyon Creek Trailhead. From the junction of U.S. Highway 39 5 and U.S. Highway 26 in downtown John Day, go south on U.S. Highway 395 (South Canyon Blvd.) for 9.8 miles. Turn left on Country Road 65, traveling 2.8 miles then turning left again on Forest Road 6510. Drive 1.6 miles to Forest Road 812; proceed 2.7 miles to the trailhead.

The hike: The following hike parallels Canyon Creek— home to lush ferns, scrumptious huckleberries, and water ouzels—for the most part, and ends high atop Indian Butte where there are wonderful views of the surrounding 68,700-acre wilderness and beyond.

Enter the wilderness almost immediately upon hiking East Canyon Creek Trail 211. You'll come to Canyon Creek in less than a mile and pass through a meadow of crimson columbine and other species in about two miles. The enormous ponderosa pines seen here are part of the Canyon Creek Research Natural Area.

Cross several creeks as you make your way to 7.6 miles where there's a good view of Indian Creek Butte.

Reach a spring and junction at 8.7 miles; take Table Mountain Trail 217, climbing a steep to moderate grade to Table Mountain Cutoff Trail 217A. Make a left, reaching an old sign at 9.4 miles. Once you pass a large rock cairn (after a very steep uphill) you'll have to hike off the trail and up the southwest slope to the top of Indian Creek Butte.

HIKE 27 *INDIAN CREEK BUTTE*

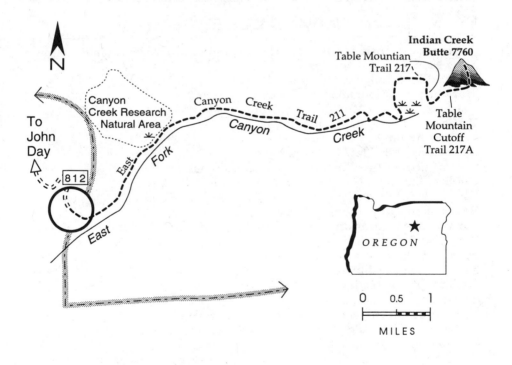

Indian Creek Butte from meadow located southwest of the Butte.

HIKE 28 *SLIDE LAKES*

General description: A round-trip day hike in the Strawberry Mountain Wilderness.
General location: Eleven miles south of Prairie City.
Maps: Prairie City 7.5-minute USGS quad; Strawberry Mountain Wilderness map.
Difficulty: Moderate.
Length: About 4.2 miles one way.

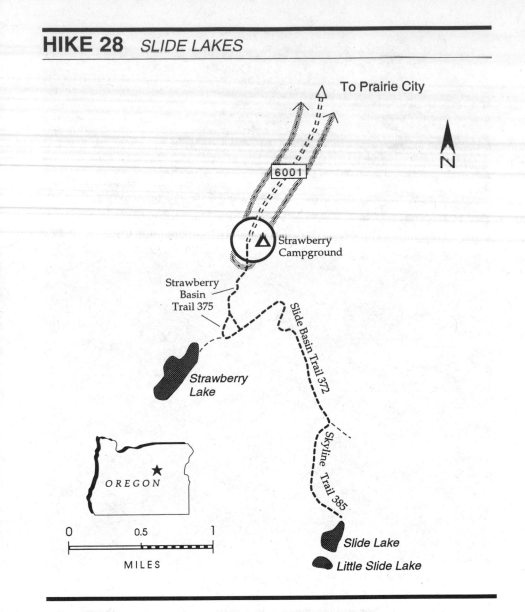

To Prairie City

N

6001

Strawberry
Campground

Strawberry
Basin
Trail 375

Slide Basin Trail 372

Strawberry
Lake

OREGON

Skyline Trail 385

0   0.5   1

MILES

Slide Lake

Little Slide Lake

Elevations: 5,770 to 6,997 feet.
Special attractions: Wildflowers, spectacular views of a glacier-carved basin, fishing at both Slide Lakes and nearby Strawberry Lake.
Water availability: See description.
Best season: July through November.
For more information: Prairie City Ranger District, Prairie City, OR 97869; (541) 820-3311.
Permit: Registration box at the trailhead.
Finding the trailhead: The trailhead begins at the Strawberry Campground, located south of Prairie City. From U.S. Highway 26, go south on Main Street,

following the signs to Bridge Street (County 60) at .4 mile. Take County 60 south for 6.6 miles to a fork; head left on Forest Road 6001, continuing four miles to the campground and trailhead.

The hike: Hike Strawberry Basin Trail 375, entering the wilderness in 200 yards. Reach the first of two Slide Lake junctions at one mile. If you'd like to visit Strawberry Lake, continue on to the lake in .2 mile. Although heavily-used, the lake is picturesque and the fishing is great.

You'll reach the second Slide Lake junction just before Strawberry Lake. Go to the left, keeping to the right upon reaching a fork (this meets up with the first junction) at 1.4 miles. Hike Slide Basin Trail 372 to a junction at 2.4 miles. Just before the junction there's a spur trail leading off to the left. From this point there's an excellent view of Slide Mountain, the Strawberry Basin, and Prairie City.

Back at the junction, keep to the right, hiking an open slope blanketed with flowers in the early summer. Come to another junction at 3.4 miles; stay to the left, now hiking Skyline Trail 385 to the Slide Lake junction at four miles. Go left, reaching 13-acre Slide Lake in .2 mile. Little Slide Lake is just over the small incline on the south end of Slide Lake. Wildflowers, including shooting stars and bull elephants head, decorate the shores of both lakes. Brook trout inhabit the two lakes as well.

HIKE 29 *SADDLE RIDGE*

General description: A round-trip day hike in the North Fork John Day Wilderness.

General location: Twenty-eight miles east of Dale.

Maps: Olive Lake 7.5-minute, Vinegar Hill 7.5-minute USGS quads; North Fork John Day Wilderness map.

Difficulty: Moderate to difficult.

Length: About 4.5 miles one way.

Elevations: 6,000 to 7,400 feet.

Special attractions: Good views; great fishing at Olive Lake.

Water availability: Several small streams en route to Saddle Ridge.

Best season: Mid-June through November.

For more information: North Fork John Day Ranger District, P.O. Box 158, Ukiah, OR 97880; (541) 427-3231.

Permit: None.

Finding the trailhead: From Dale, drive twenty-seven miles east on Forest Road 10. Turn right on Forest Road 480 where you'll see a sign to Olive Lake. Drive to roads end and the trailhead in one mile.

The hike: The 121,111-acre North Fork John Day Wilderness is divided into four distinct units, all of varying sizes. From the smallest to the largest, the units are as follows: Tower, Baldy Creek, Greenhorn, and the North Fork John Day. This trail follows the western edge of the Greenhorn Unit, located in the Greenhorn Mountains.

Hike Saddle Camp Trail 3035, an old road, crossing a creek as you ascend to Upper Olive Lake, a dry lake now serving mostly as a meadow. The lake

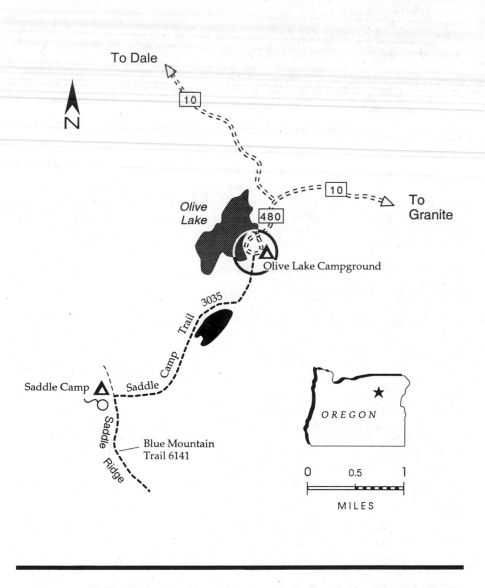

To Dale

N

10

Olive
Lake

480

10 - - - ▷ To
Granite

Olive Lake Campground

3035

Saddle Camp Trail

Saddle Camp ▲ Saddle

Saddle
Ridge

Blue Mountain
Trail 6141

OREGON

★

0   0.5   1

MILES

was dammed at one time and used in association with the Fremont Power Plant.

Constructed in 1907, the Fremont Powerhouse Pipeline was built to generate electrical power to nearby Granite (which was a thriving town at that time). Surrounding mines would also benefit. Small when compared to today's modern plants, it was the largest structure in the region at that time. Built for about $100,000., the plant measured roughly eighty-three feet by twenty-eight feet. Horse-drawn wagons transported all material and machinery from

Baker. Although it last generated electrical power in 1967, it is now a historic site with a place on the National Register of Historic Places.

Cross into the wilderness upon reaching the end of the road trail at 1.4 miles. Continue on a standard trail to Saddle Camp and the junction of Blue Mountain Trail 6141 in less than three miles. Go south (left) and up the hill for a good view of Upper Olive Lake at 3.3 miles. You'll pass through a burn area (the result of a series of lightning strikes in 1986) as you proceed along Saddle Ridge. There is another good view of both Olive Lakes and the surrounding areas at 4.5 miles.

HIKE 30 NORTH FORK JOHN DAY RIVER

General description: A three- to four-day round-trip backpack in the North Fork John Day Wilderness.
General location: Fifty miles east of Baker.
Maps: Trout Meadows 7.5-minute, Silver Butte 7.5-minute, Olive Lake 7.5-minute USGS quads; North Fork John Day Wilderness map.
Difficulty: Moderate.
Length: About 13.7 miles one way.
Elevations: 5,200 to 3,936 feet.
Special attractions: Great fishing, wildlife, solitude except in the fall when hunters abound.

Cabin along the North Fork John Day River.

Water availability: Plentiful along the entire trail.
Best season: Mid-June through November.
For more information: North Fork John Day Ranger District, P.O. Box 158, Ukiah, OR 97880; (541) 427-3231.
Permit: None.
Finding the trailhead: The trailhead begins 8.5 miles north of the small town of Granite, at a campground near the junction of Forest Road 52 and Forest Road 73.

The hike: Hike North Fork Trail 3022, entering the wilderness in about 100 feet. Ford the North Fork John Day River then hike parallel to the river, watching for miners' cabins along the way. Some of the cabins are open to the public. The owners, however, ask that you leave things as they were when you arrived. If things are a bit on the messy side, clean it up, leaving the place cleaner than you found it.

As you walk the trail you're bound to see a variety of jars nailed to trees, usually at about eye level. Inside each jar you'll find a photocopy of a mining claim. In the mid- to late-1800s, this region was bustling with miners searching

HIKE 30 *NORTH FORK JOHN DAY RIVER*

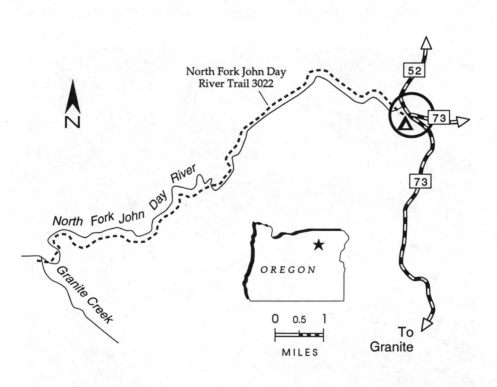

for gold and silver. Miners left with roughly $10 million in gold and silver.

Around five miles you'll pass the Thornburg Placer Mine, obviously a potpourri of mining activity at one time. You'll pass an old cabin on the right in less than two more miles. Keep straight when a sign states that this is Trail 6041. It is still Trail 3022.

Soon after passing a sign "Whisker Peak" at 10.6 miles, you'll see a cabin on the left. Hike the spur trail leading past the cabin, then ford the river, continuing on the opposite side to a sign "Bear Gulch" in another .2 mile. If you continue past the cabin on the main trail, you'll find a deep ford ahead of you.

Reach Granite Creek and some horse corrals at 13.7 miles. Anglers may want to take a break and cast in a line. The North Fork John Day River and its tributaries provide almost forty miles of prime spawning habitat for anadromous

Hiker (Donna) and her dog (Sam) at Nip and Tuck Pass.

and resident fish. Dolly Varden, rainbow and brook trout, as well as a native run of Chinook salmon inhabit these scenic waters.

Although the North Fork John Day River Trail (a National Recreation Trail) extends for miles along the bountiful North Fork John Day River, this guide describes the route to the confluence of Granite Creek.

HIKE 31 *LOST LAKE SADDLE*

General description: A long round-trip day hike or a two-day round-trip backpack in the North Fork John Day Wilderness.
General location: Thirty-three miles northwest of Baker.
Maps: Anthony Lakes 7.5-minutes USGS quad.
Difficulty: Moderate.
Length. About 6.2 miles one way.
Elevations: 7,131 to 8,100 feet.
Special attractions: Wonderful views, wildlife.
Water availability: None on trail, although two lakes—Black and Dutch Flat—are located off the trail.
Best season: Mid- to late-June through November.
For more information: Baker Ranger District, Rt. 1, Box 1, Baker, OR 97814; (541) 523-4476.
Permit: None.
Finding the trailhead: Reach the Elkhorn Crest Trailhead by driving west from Haines on County 411 (which later turns into Forest Road 73), following the signs to Anthony Lake. The signed trailhead is located just before reaching the campground turnoff, twenty-four miles from Haines.

The hike: The 121,111-acre North Fork John Day Wilderness is different than most other preserves as it is divided into four distinct sections, ranging in size from 8,073 acres to over 85,000 acres. You'll reach Lost Lake Saddle by hiking a portion of the Elkhorn Crest National Recreation Trail which rests in the Baldy Creek unit. The granite peaks of the Elkhorn Mountain Range make this one of the most beautiful of all the units.

Begin climbing Elkhorn Crest Trail 1611, passing a junction to Black Lake along the way. Stunted, twisted pines, born among granite slopes, decorate the land as you climb to the wilderness boundary at 2.9 miles.

You'll travel from one saddle to the next as you make your way to Nip and Tuck Pass at 5.4 miles. Along the way there are wonderful views of the surrounding region. From the Lost Lake Saddle at 6.2 miles, there are views of Mt. Hood and several other large Cascade peaks to the west.

The trail follows the Elkhorn Crest along the eastern boundary of the Baldy Creek unit, a high ridge dressed in a subalpine forest of whitebark pine, lodgepole pine, and subalpine fir. Look for various types of wildlife in this region. Elk bugle in the fall. Also, there are deer, black bear, and mountain lion. On occasion someone reports seeing a mountain goat. The Forest Service transported a small herd of sixteen from both Alaska and Olympic National Parks during the past few years.

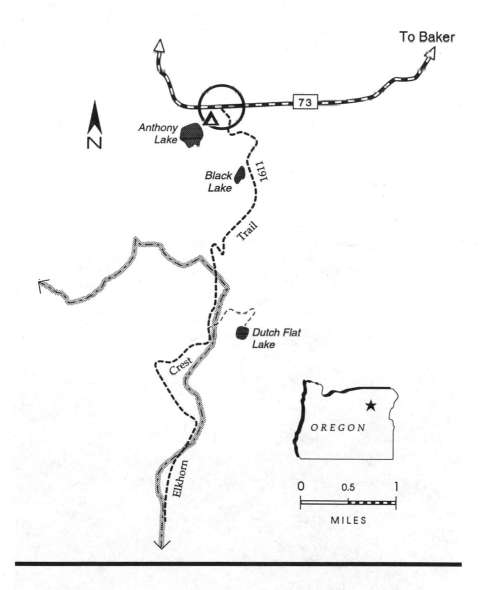

To Baker

N

73

Anthony
Lake

Black
Lake

1611

Trail

Dutch Flat
Lake

Crest

Elkhorn

OREGON

★

0   0.5   1

MILES

HIKE 32 *TRAVERSE LAKE*

General description: A long round-trip day hike or a two-day round-trip backpack in the Eagle Cap Wilderness.
General location: About forty-two miles southeast of La Grande.
Maps: Bennet Peak 7.5-minute USGS quad; Eagle Cap Wilderness map.
Difficulty: Moderate.
Length: About 7.3 miles one way.
Elevations: 5,570 to 7,760 feet.
Special attractions: Grand views, wildflowers, good fishing and swimming.
Water availability: See description.
Best season: July through October.
For more information: Eagle Cap Ranger District, P.O. Box M, Enterprise, OR 97828; (541) 426-3104.
Permit: None.
Finding the trailhead: From the small town of Union, about fourteen miles southeast of La Grande, drive south on Oregon 203 for thirteen miles. Turn left onto Forest Road 77, traveling another 14.3 miles to West Eagle Meadow. (Road 77 is well-maintained gravel for the first ten miles, a rough dirt road after that. Although a sign attempts to deter those with passenger cars, we saw many small cars parked at the trailhead.) Turn left, reaching the trailhead .3 mile down the road.

Echo Lake, photograph taken from the ridge near Traverse Lake.

HIKE 32 *TRAVERSE LAKE*

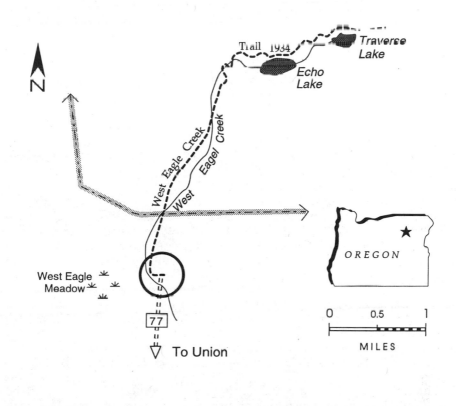

The hike: The Eagle Cap Wilderness is a land of alpine lakes and meadows, steep glaciated valleys, splendid vistas, and ample wildlife. Comprised of 358,461 acres, Eagle Cap is Oregon's largest wilderness (and one of the most popular) with more than 500 miles of trails penetrating the preserve.

Hike West Eagle Creek Trail 1934, entering the wilderness in .1 mile. Cross Fake Creek and several other small streams before crossing West Eagle Creek at .8 mile. Although the trail appears to continue following the creek, it doesn't. Ford the creek, crossing through a meadow and then along an open slope where wildflowers abound in the summer months.

There's a creek at 2.2 miles—your last chance for water for several miles. Reach the junction of Trail 1943 in another one-half mile. Turn right at the sign reading "Trail Creek." Switchback up to West Eagle Creek at less than five miles.

You'll pass an unnamed lake and Echo Lake as you continue to Traverse Lake. The thirty-one-acre lake is stocked with eastern brook trout.

HIKE 33 *LOOKINGGLASS LAKE*

General description: A long round-trip day hike or a two-day round-trip backpack in the Eagle Cap Wilderness.
General location: About forty miles northeast of Baker.
Maps: Bennet Peak 7.5-minute USGS quad; Eagle Cap Wilderness map.
Difficulty: Moderate to steep.
Length: About 7.4 miles one way.
Elevations: 5,231 to 7,360 feet.
Special attractions: Wildflowers, spectacular views, and one of the most beautiful lakes imaginable with Needlepoint Mountain providing a splendid backdrop.
Water availability: See description.
Best season: July through October.
For more information: Eagle Cap Ranger District, P.O. Box M, Enterprise, OR 97828; (541) 426-3104.
Permit: None.
Finding the trailhead: To reach the trailhead drive from Medical Springs, a tiny town about twenty-three miles northeast of Baker. Turn right in Medical Springs, heading south on Collins Road for 1.6 miles then left on Forest Road 67. Travel Road 67 for thirteen miles to Forest Road 77; turn left reaching a fork in .7 mile. Make a right, driving Forest Road 7755 for 3.7 miles to the trailhead.

The hike: The Eagle Cap Wilderness rests in the Wallowa Mountains, a spur of the Blue Mountains of northeast Oregon. First established in 1940 when the Secretary of Agriculture set aside 220,000 acres, Eagle Cap later became part of the National Wilderness Preservation System under the Wilderness Act of 1964. Today, Oregon's largest wilderness contains 358,461 acres.

The trailhead is located at the old Boulder Creek Resort. Just across the way you'll see a huge slide which occurred in the spring of 1984. The earth slipped down the mountain, gliding across the creek, and up to Boulder Resort. Remarkably, the creek bed remained boulder-free.

Main Eagle Creek Trail 1922 travels through the trees then across Eagle Creek at .3 mile. Cross a small stream and enter the wilderness at 1.5 miles. There are several other stream crossings as you make your way past Copper Creek Falls to a junction at 2.8 miles.

Stay to the right on Trail 1922, following the sign "Trail Creek," to Lookingglass Lake. There's another stream crossing before entering a gorgeous valley and a junction at 4.3 miles. Head right then ford Eagle Creek before climbing the moderate to steep grade to a junction at 5.3 miles. Go right on unmarked Trail 1921, crossing several more streams before reaching Lookingglass Lake at 7.4 miles.

Although plenty deep for swimming, the lake is too cold for all except those hardy souls capable of withstanding frigid waters. Anglers may hook eastern brook, brook, and cutthroat trout.

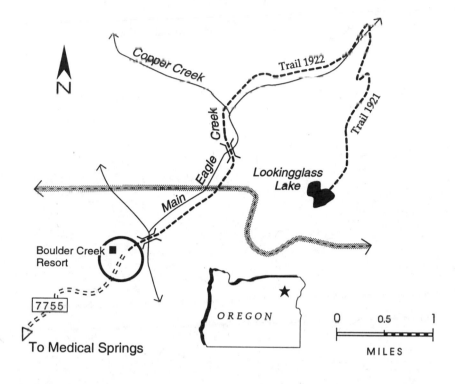

HIKE 34 *HIDDEN LAKE*

General description: A long round-trip day hike or a two- to three-day round-trip backpack in the Eagle Cap Wilderness.

General location: Approximately fifty miles northeast of Baker.

Maps: Krag Peak 7.5-minute USGS quad; Eagle Cap Wilderness map.

Difficulty: Moderate to difficult.

Length: About nine miles one way.

Elevations: 4,400 to 7,280 feet.

Special attractions: Alpine lakes, flower-filled meadows, pika, good fishing.

Water availability: East Eagle Creek, Hidden Lake, and several other small creeks.

Best season: July through October

For more information: Eagle Cap Ranger District, P.O. Box M, Enterprise, OR 97828; (541) 426-3104.

Permit: None.

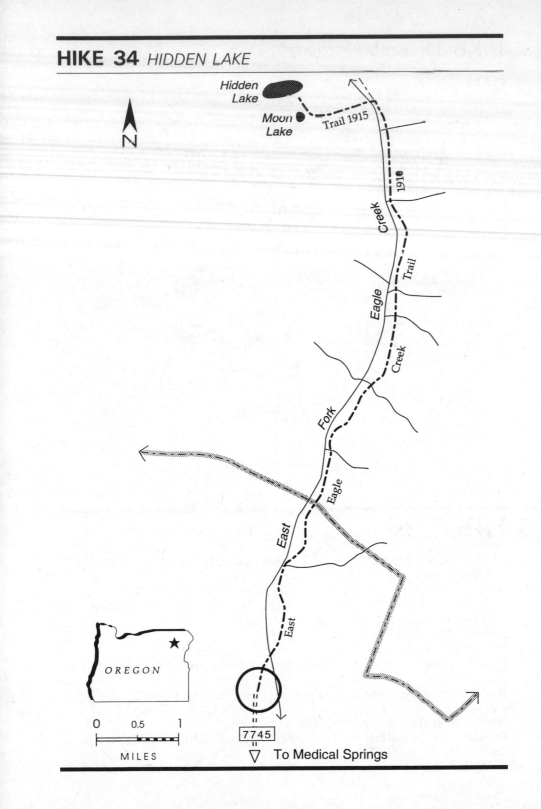

Hidden
Lake

Moon
Lake

Trail 1915

Creek

1910

Eagle

Trail

Creek

Fork

Eagle

East

Eagle

East

N

OREGON

0   0.5   1

MILES

7745

To Medical Springs

Finding the trailhead: Reach the East Eagle Creek Trailhead by driving to Medical Springs via Oregon 203. Turn right (south) on Collins Road. The road is bumpy at times, but in fairly good shape otherwise. At 1.6 miles you'll come to a fork; turn left on Forest Road 67. Reach a second fork after driving another thirteen miles. Go right on Forest Road 77 for six miles to Forest Road 7745. (Although the Forest Service map claims this is Forest Road 7740, it is actually Forest Road 7745.) Head to the left on Road 7745, driving about 5.8 miles to the trailhead.

The hike. Go north on the East Eagle Creek Trail 1910, following the drainage past Pappy's mine, crossing several small streams along the way. There are good views of the mountains to the north and northeast while hiking much of the trail.

Look for a signpost about seven miles. Although the post was there when we last checked, the sign was missing. Ford East Eagle Creek, climbing the steep slope via Trail 1915 for over a mile until reaching Moon Lake. Hidden Lake is around the north end of the lake, over another steep ridge, and past a small stream. Eastern brook trout live in this scenic lake.

Hidden Lake.

HIKE 35 McGRAW CREEK LOOP

General description: A long day hike or a two-day backpack in the Hells Canyon Wilderness and the 652,488-acre Hells Canyon National Recreation Area.

General location: About eighty miles east of Baker.

Maps: Homestead 7.5-minute USGS quad; Hells Canyon Wilderness map.

Difficulty: Moderate to steep.

Length: Approximately fourteen miles.

Elevations: 1,760 to 3,360 feet.

Special attractions: Close-up view of Hells Canyon, the Snake River, and an old homestead. Also, an abundance of wild flowers and wildlife.

Water availability: See description.

Best season: Usually open all year, but is closed on occasion due to snow.

For more information: Hells Canyon National Recreation Area, P.O. Box 490, Enterprise, OR 97828; (541) 426-3151.

Permit: None.

Finding the trailhead: To reach the trailhead from Baker, drive Oregon 86 east for seventy miles. Turn left on County Road 1039—driving past beautiful Copperfield Park Campground—for nine miles until it ends at the trailhead.

The hike: Hells Canyon isn't just the deepest gorge in North America, it's "the deepest canyon in low relief territory," according to the 1991 Guinness Book of World Records. From its highest point atop Devil Mountain to its lowest on the Snake River—the dividing line between Oregon and Idaho—Hells Canyon plunges 7,900 feet.

A word of caution for those who are allergic to poison oak. Unfortunately, the vine is prolific along the lower reaches of this loop. Animal life is also abundant: look for kingfishers, chukars, and elk to name a few.

Begin hiking Hells Canyon Trail 1890 along the lower reaches of the Snake River Canyon. You'll cross several streams in route .

Reach a junction to the return trail (McGraw Creek Trail 1879) in about two miles. Continue on less than a mile to Bench Trail 1884 where you'll head to the left and up the slope. (You'll pass into the Hells Canyon National Recreation Area and Wilderness near this point.)

Cross Spring Creek before the four-mile mark. The trail is somewhat obscured in this area as dense vegetation has covered much of it. Look for an occasional rock cairn to help lead the way. Later, a series of steep switchbacks lead to a signed junction at 5.6 miles. Turn onto the McGraw Cabin Trail 1879 just before the sign.

Cross another stream at 5.9 miles and Spring Creek again at 6.7 miles. A grove of stately ponderosa pines rest on private property at 7.4 miles. Reach McGraw Cabin at 9.3 miles.

The Luther Perkins family first rode into the area fifty-eight years ago. They traveled up McGraw Creek, homesteaded this beautiful chunk of land, and built the cabin seen today. According to the Forest Service, Perkins raised turkeys on his land, herding them down to Baker at sale time.

There are two trails leading from the cabin. Do not hike to the creek, instead go to the left of the fence, following the trail that runs along

HIKE 35 *McGRAW CREEK LOOP*

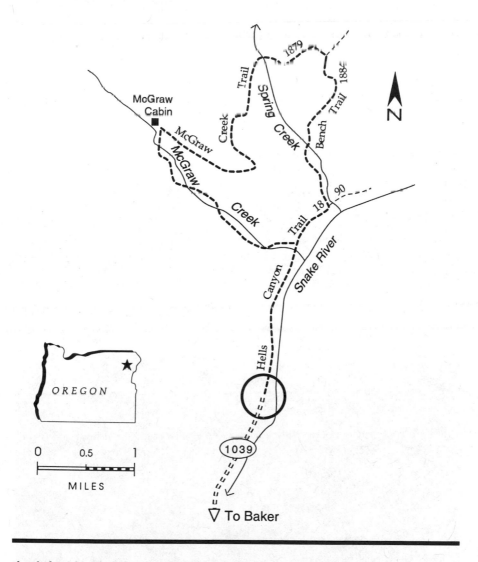

the left side of the creek. Ford the McGraw Creek at 10.1 miles.

There are several creek crossings, all sans bridges, as you descend through this scenic area. Reach the junction of the Hells Canyon Trail at 12.1 miles. Turn right to head back to the trailhead.

HIKE 36 *HELLS CANYON LOOP*

General description: A three- to five-day loop backpack in the Hells Canyon Wilderness and National Recreation Area.

General location: Approximately forty-six miles east of Joseph.

Maps: Hat Point 7.5-minute, Old Timer Mountain 7.5-minute USGS quads; Hells Canyon National Recreation Area map.

Difficulty: Moderate to difficult.

Length: About thirty miles.

Elevations: 1,345 to 5,360 feet.

Special attractions: Wide vistas of Hells Canyon, the deepest gorge in North America, abundant wildlife including elk, and wildflowers.

Water availability: See description.

Best season: May through November, however, lower portions of the trail are snowfree most of the year.

For more information: Hells Canyon National Recreation Area, P.O. Box 490, Enterprise, OR 97828; (541) 426-3151.

Permit: None.

Finding the trailhead: The trail begins at the Freezeout Trailhead. From Oregon 82 and Wallowa Road in Joseph, drive east on Wallowa Road for thirty miles to Imnaha. Make a right on Upper Imnaha Road (County 727) and travel 12.7 miles; go left on Forest Road 4230, reaching the trailhead in three miles.

The hike: This loop is typical of the Hells Canyon Wilderness: Habitat is varied—steep and rugged one minute, gentle the next—draped in trees at times,

Horsemen off the Sluice Creek Trail.

open to the scorching sun at others. Several special notes: poison oak exists along the lower reaches of both Saddle and Sluice creeks, as well as the Snake River; watch for rattlesnakes; be prepared for a lot of elevation gain and loss.

Hike Saddle Creek Trail 1776, climbing the open slope to the junction of Western Rim Recreation Trail 1774 (known also as the Summit Trail) at 2.2 miles. Pass into the wilderness at this point, then begin descending the Saddle Creek drainage. Although the trail runs parallel to the creek, water can be difficult to reach due to thick brush and downed trees from a 1973 fire. Fortunately, you'll cross several creeks along the way to the Snake River at 9.5 miles.

Go north along the mighty Snake via the Snake River Trail 1726. Shade is scarce now, with extreme heat prevalent in the summer. Reach Sluice Creek at 14.5 miles.

Head up Sluice Creek Trail 1748, hiking through dense vegetation before heading up and away from the creek. Now an occasional stand of trees provides the only shade. Hike the High Trail 1751 at 18.3 miles, going .2 mile to Hat Creek and the junction to Hat Point.

Although this loop continues along High Trail, I'd recommend a side trip to 6,982-foot Hat Point. To do so, hike Hat Creek Trail 1752 to Hat Point,

HIKE 36 HELLS CANYON LOOP

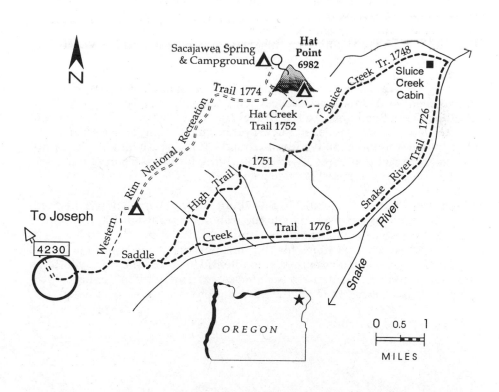

an additional 3.7 miles and 2,300 feet up. The trail may seem an easy hike, especially after hiking up from the Snake River.

From Hat Point, you'll look down more than a mile into Hells Canyon. Those who would rather take a shortcut can hike Forest Roads 332, 315, and 4240. (These roads also serve as the Western Rim National Recreation Trail 1774.) Just past the Saddle Creek Campground, head left on Trail 1774, hiking to Freezeout Saddle, and back to the trailhead in 9.6 miles.

Back at the High Trail junction, continue on High Trail 1751 (a sign reads No. 418). Cross several creeks en route to the junction of Saddle Creek Trail at twenty-six miles. Go west on Saddle Creek Trail 1776 which leads to the trailhead.

HIKE 37 *NINEMILE RIDGE*

General description: A long round-trip day hike or a two-day round-trip backpack in the North Fork Umatilla Wilderness.
General location: Thirty miles east of Pendleton.
Maps: Andies Prairie 7.5-minute, Bingham Springs 7.5-minute USGS quads.
Difficulty: Moderate.
Length: About 6.8 miles one way.
Elevations: 2,400 to 5,100 feet.
Special attractions: Magnificent views, solitude (except in the fall when hunters descend upon the area), wildlife, wildflowers.
Water availability: None.
Best season: June through November.
For more information: Umatilla National Forest, 2517 S.W. Hailey, Pendleton, OR 97801; (541) 276-3811.
Permit: None.
Finding the trailhead: From the junction of Oregon 82 and Oregon 204 in Elgin, head west on Oregon 204, driving 3.8 miles to Forest Road 3738 (Phillips Creek Road); make a left. Travel 10.5 miles to Forest Road 31; make another left, going 3.8 miles to Ruckel Junction. Go right on Forest Road 32 for 10.2 miles to the Umatilla Campground. At the south end off the campground, turn right on Forest Road 415, driving until it ends in .2 mile. The trailhead is near the Forest Service gate.

The hike: Ninemile Trail 3072 begins about 100 yards or so down the road. You'll see some dirt steps leading to the trail and a trail sign 100 feet off the road. You'll enter the wilderness in .1 mile.

The grade is steep at times for the first portion of the trail, but then it levels off some as you hike across Ninemile Ridge . From the ridge you'll see that the 20,144-acre wilderness is a land of extremely steep, timbered canyons, and plateaus decorated with native bunchgrass and an occasional tree.

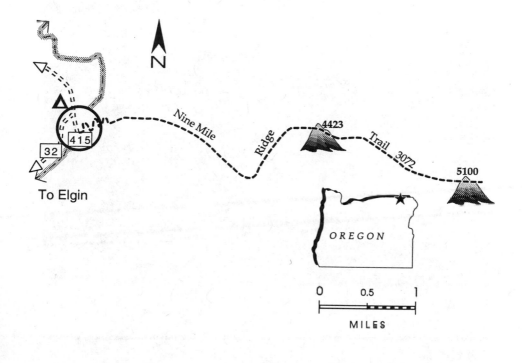

To Elgin

OREGON

0   0.5   1

MILES

Day hiker on the trail from Elk Flat to the Wenaha River.

HIKE 38 *WEHAHAH RIVER*

General description: A round-trip day hike or a two- day round-trip back-pack in the Wenaha-Tucannon Wilderness.
General location: Approximately fifty-five miles north of La Grande.
Maps: Wenaha Forks 7.5-minute USGS quad; Wenaha-Tucannon Wilderness map.
Difficulty: Moderate.
Length: About 4.5 miles one way.
Elevations: 4,900 to 3,000 feet.
Special attractions: Solitude (except during hunting season), wildlife including bald and golden eagles and other birds of prey, woodpeckers, and various mammals.
Water availability: Wenaha River.
Best season: June through November.

For more information: Umatilla National Forest, 2517 S.W. Hailey Avenue, Pendleton, OR 97801; (541) 276-3811.
Permit: None.
Finding the trailhead: Reach the Elk Flat Trailhead by driving from the small town of Troy, south toward Long Meadow. The road forks at .9 mile; head right to Long Meadow on Forest Road 62 (Lookingglass-Troy Road). Go 20.2 miles to a signed dirt road leading to Elk Flat. Drive .7 mile to the trailhead.

The hike: Unlike many hiking trails, this one begins at a high point and descends to the river below. Although several trails lead to the Wenaha River, this is perhaps one of the nicest. You'll hike through the trees, yet there are open areas for a look into other portions of the wilderness.

Hike Elk Flat Trail 3241, entering the wilderness immediately upon descending the moderate grade through mature timber to the confluence of the South Fork and North Fork Wenaha Rivers below. If you'd like to do some additional hiking in the 177,412-acre preserve, the Wenaha River Trail 6144 is located on the opposite side of the river. Cross near the washed-out bridge and continue until you reach the well-maintained trail.

This region was first inhabited by Native Americans. In fact, most of the trails in the Blue Mountain Range originated from paths chosen by the natives. Elk hunters make the greatest use of the trails today.

HIKE 38 *WEHAHA RIVER*

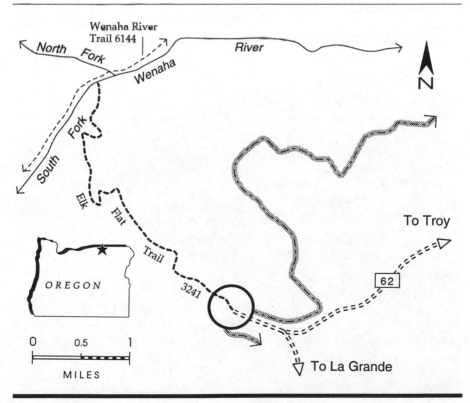

HIKE 39 *MT. HOWARD*

General description: A short loop day hike in the Wallowa-Whitman National Forest.

General location: About six miles south of Joseph, twelve miles south of Enterprise.

Maps: Joseph 15-minute USGS quad.

Difficulty: Easy.

Length: About two miles.

Elevations: 8,100 to 8,256 feet.

Special attractions: Amazing close-up views of the Eagle Cap Wilderness with portions of four states visible on clear days.

Water availability: Snack bar and restrooms located on top of Mt. Howard.

Best season: Late May through early October.

For more information: Wallowa Valley Ranger District, Rt. 1, Box 83, Joseph, OR 97846; (541) 432-2171.

Permit: None, although you will need to buy a ticket for the Wallowa Lake Tramway which will transport you to the top of Mt. Howard.

Finding the trailhead: From downtown Joseph (all services), go south on Oregon 82, passing beautiful Wallowa Lake en route. At 5.9 miles reach a fork; go left for .3 mile to the gondola. There are two state park campgrounds (both charge a fee) nearby. Also there are shops, lodging, and restaurants in this area.

View of the Eagle Cap Wilderness from atop Mt. Howard.

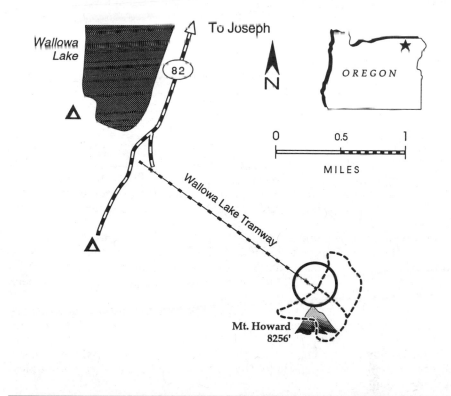

The hike: Unlike most of the trails in this book, this loop trail gets a lot of use. Why include it in this book then? Because it's a wonderful hike for families or those limited to short hikes. It's for youngsters and oldsters and everyone in between. It's even for experienced backpackers in need of a day of rest and a quick ride to a never-ending chain of splendid views.

The hike begins with a ride up the Wallowa Lake Tramway. For a price, you'll travel 3,700 feet in about fifteen minutes. Has hiking ever been so easy?

Reach Mt. Howard then ooh and aah your way to several splendid lookouts. There's no need to guide you around the summit as trails are easy to follow and well-defined. There are about two miles of trails, with restrooms at the tram area (along with a snack bar/deli), and pit toilets near two overlooks.

HIKE 40 HUCKLEBERRY MOUNTAIN

General description: A round-trip day hike in the Wallowa-Whitman National Forest.

General location: About fourteen miles south of the small town of Wallowa.

Maps: Enterprise 15-minute USGS quad.

Difficulty: Difficult.

Length: About 2.5 miles one way.

Elevations: 5,600 to 7,552 feet.

Special attractions: Spectacular views, solitude, wildflowers.

Water availability: Spring at two miles, though I'd carry water.

Best season: July through October.

For more information: Wallowa-Whitman National Forest, P.O. Box 907, Baker City, OR 97814; (541) 523-6391.

Permit: None.

Finding the trailhead: To reach the trailhead from Wallowa, a small town with all services, go west on Oregon 82 to First Street in about .3 mile. A sign points the way to Bear Creek Road which you'll reach in another .4 mile; go left. The road is paved but turns to gravel after 2.2 miles. Later it changes to Forest Road 8250.

After traveling seven miles from First Street reach a fork; go left, continuing on Forest Road 8250 (now called Bear Saddle Road), an unmaintained road. Although a sign recommends that passenger cars refrain from using the road, we found the road in fine shape, easily managed by passenger cars. Check with the Forest Service for current conditions.

If you need a campground, go right at the fork for .8 mile to Boundary Camp, a free campground along Bear Creek, with picnic tables, fire pits, outhouses.

Travel another seven miles from this fork to the trailhead which is at another fork, on the right hand side. The trailhead isn't the easiest to see unless you are looking for it.

The hike: If you like to climb, gaining elevation as quickly as possible, then you'll enjoy this steep trail. The reward? Tremendous views from atop Huckleberry Mountain.

Begin hiking Huckleberry Mountain Trail 1667 which follows a road (unmarked Forest Road 160), crossing the road and continuing along the opposite side. The trail climbs and descends at a moderate grade, heading back to the road at .4 mile. Cross a small stream then head up the trail which begins climbing at a very steep grade. If you'd rather park here you can, although space is limited. Those with horses will want to park at the first trailhead. This trail is open to hikers and horse people, but not to bikes and motorized vehicles.

The trail is very steep with loose pebbles a problem in the first mile. Steep switchbacks make the going somewhat easier (it won't feel like much) after the first mile or so. Reach a camp and spring at 2.1 miles. Now the grade eases up as you continue to the summit and site of an old lookout at 2.5 miles.

From the summit and various points along the ridge, you'll see 360 degrees to Enterprise and the Wallowa Valley below, and you'll gaze upon many

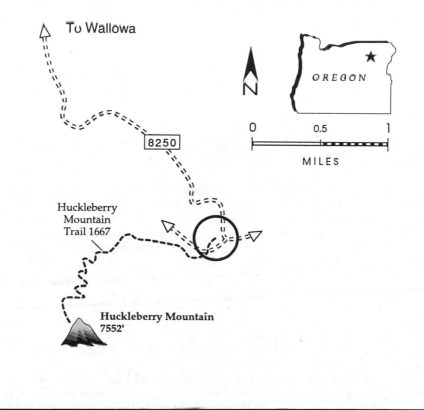

high mountain peaks of the Eagle Cap Wilderness. In fact, from this point you're on the northern border of the Eagle Cap Wilderness, a magnificent place to hike. Also, there are tremendous views into the Bear Creek and Lostine River drainages.

HIKE 41 SAWTOOTH CRATER

General description: A short day hike in the Wallowa-Whitman National Forest.
General location: About thirty-two miles northeast of Baker City.
Maps: Sawtooth Ridge 7.5-minute USGS quad.
Difficulty: Easy to moderate.
Length: About .7 mile one way.
Elevations: 4,680 to 5,171 feet.
Special attractions: Spectacular views and an indepth look at a volcano crater. The trail is currently unmaintained due to lack of use. If you want solitude, this is the place!
Water availability: None.
Best season: May through November.
For more information: La Grande Ranger District, 3502 Highway 30, La Grande, OR 97850; (541) 963-7186.
Permit: None.
Finding the trailhead: The unmaintained trail is located northeast of Baker City (all services). Take Interstate 84 about seven miles to the north then head east on Oregon 203. Travel 18.1 miles to Medical Springs and go right on Collins Road. Go another 1 .7 miles to a fork; continue right on Collins Road (Forest Road 70). You'll pass an interpretative sign for Sawtooth Crater after going an additional 4.7 miles. The trailhead is just ahead .6 mile. Forest Road 740 leads to the trail but it's easier to park off Road 70 and walk Road 740 as there is no room to park.

The hike: Although small portions of this trail are steep, it's a good hike for families because it's short and scenic. A perfect place for packing a lunch and eating atop the crater, you'll sit on what is a vent plug of an ancient volcano.

Begin hiking unmaintained Road 740 through the trees for .1 mile. A sign points the way to the trail which reverts back to a road and then back again to a standard trail. Signs help lead the way as you pass through the forest. The grade is moderate as you hike up (sometimes via switchback) to a ridge at .6 mile. Scramble up the steep rocky slope to the left and the summit at .7 mile.

There's a great view of the nearby Wallowa Mountains, the Blue Mountains (Elkhorn Ridge), and Baker Valley.

If you read the interpretative sign before hiking the trail, you'll find that the peak is actually a 420-foot plug. After hiking up to the top of the crater, you'll see both halves of the crater and the central "sawtooth ridge," thus the name. Spanning a total of 650 acres, the crater is nearly one mile from rim-to-rim, and it is about 400 feet deep. The central plug reaches 420 feet from the base to the heavens.

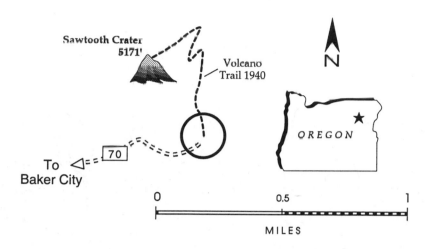

HIKE 42 *THE LAKES LOOKOUT*

General description: A short day hike in the Elkhorn Mountains of eastern Oregon.
General location: About forty miles northwest of Baker City.
Maps: Anthony Lakes 7.5-minute USGS quad.
Difficulty: Moderate.
Length: About two miles one way.
Elevations: 7,800 to 8,522 feet.
Special attractions: Grand views of the Anthony Lakes and Crawfish Basin, as well as tremendous close-up views of the magnificent Elkhorn Range.
Water availability: None.
Best season: July through October.
For more information: Wallowa-Whitman National Forest, P.O. Box 907, Baker City, OR 97814; (541) 523-6391.
Permit: None.

HIKE 42 *THE LAKES LOOKOUT*

To Baker City

73

210

N

★

OREGON

MILES

0   0.5   1

The lakes
Lookout
8522'

Finding the trailhead: To reach the trail from Haines (cafes, market, gas), located about ten miles northwest of Baker City on U.S. 30, go west on County Road 1146. A sign points the way to Anthony Lakes. County Road 1146 turns into Forest Road 73 along the way, all while climbing up into the mountains. Pass Anthony Lake Campground after traveling 23.7 miles from Haines. A fee is charged.

Continue past the Anthony Lakes Campground for another 3.8 miles then make a left onto Forest Road 210, a unmaintained dirt road (passenger cars okay), and travel two miles to the trailhead.

The hike: If you enjoy hiking in alpine areas where trees are stunted and wildflowers profuse, where granitic rock types give the entire country a rugged look, where views are neverending, then you'll have to hike this trail.

From the site of an old lookout, you'll gaze down upon the Anthony Lakes Basin, Crawfish Basin, and you'll see east to the Wallowa Mountains, and south into some of the North Fork John Day Wilderness.

View of the North Fork John Day Wilderness from Lakes Lookout.

Begin hiking an old road which soon turns into a steep trail. Reach the summit of the easy-to-follow trail at one mile. As mentioned previously, there are fantastic views from this point.

HIKE 43 *BLACK CANYON*

General description: A two- to three-day round-trip backpack in the Black Canyon Wilderness.
General location: About fifty-seven miles east of Prineville, thirty-five miles west of John Day.
Maps: Wolf Mountain, Aldrich Gulch 7.5-minute USGS quads.
Difficulty: Moderate to difficult.
Length: About 11.6 miles one-way.
Elevations: 6,400 to 2,850 feet.
Special attractions: Mature forest of Douglas-fir and ponderosa pine, solitude, and wildflowers in the late spring/early summer.
Water availability: Water is readily available throughout the entire hike.
Best season: June through November.
For more information: Paulina Ranger District, 171500 Beaver Creek Rd., Paulina, OR 97751, (541) 477-3713.
Permit: None.
Finding the trailhead: Drive U.S. Highway 26 to Forest Road 12, located

sixty-three miles east of Prineville and fourteen miles west of Dayville. Turn right (south) on Forest Road 12 for 15.6 miles; make a left on Forest Road 1250. After 3.9 miles head straight at the junction, now driving Forest Road 090. Although rocky, the road is passable for passenger cars in good weather. Drive 3.6 miles then turn left on Forest Road 5820. Continue .4 mile to Forest Road 5840 and drive this road 2.5 miles to the trailhead.

The hike: This is a wonderful hike if you don't mind getting your feet wet. Black Canyon Creek flows from west to east through the wilderness for which it was named, plunging more than 3,000 feet before emptying into the South Fork John Day River.

Black Canyon Trail 820 descends at a gradual, sometimes steep grade past Owl Creek and on to Black Canyon Creek at just over three miles. Along the way, ferns, flowers and trees make the hike interesting.

You'll cross Black Canyon Creek and numerous other streams as you descend to about six miles. Now the trail climbs moderately, heading up and

HIKE 43 *BLACK CANYON*

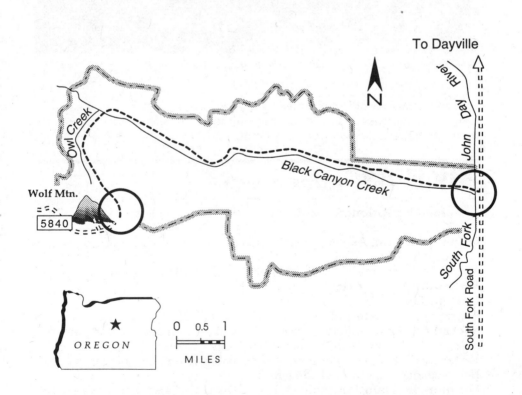

around the steep slope below. Continue hiking through the water and on dry land to the South Fork John Day River.

If you have access to a shuttle on South Fork Road, ford the river and your hike is complete. Look for this trailhead off South Fork Road approximately thirteen miles south of Dayville. (This trailhead is also fine for those who'd rather hike the trail in reverse, gaining altitude the first day instead of descending.)

Numerous species of animal life inhabit the preserve. The Forest Service boasts of 300 species on their lands, many of which live in the wilderness. Although most are shy and difficult to observe, I saw several rattlesnakes while hiking the trail.

Hiker at Arch Rock.

HIKE 44 ARCH ROCK

General description: A short day hike in the Malheur National Forest.
General location: About thirty miles northeast of John Day.
Maps: Susanville 15-minute USGS quad.
Difficulty: Easy.
Length: About .3 mile one way.
Elevations: 4,200 to 4,400 feet.
Special attractions: Excellent close-up view of a natural arch rock; solitude, wildflowers.
Water availability: None.
Best season: April through November.
For more information: Bear Valley Ranger District, 528 Main St., John Day, OR 97845; (541) 575-2110.
Permit: None.
Finding the trailhead: From John Day (where you'll find all services), go

HIKE 44 ARCH ROCK

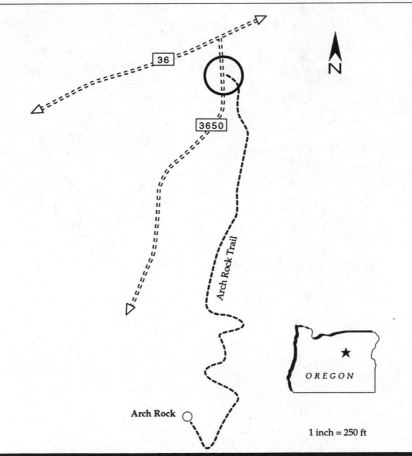

east on U.S. 26 for 9.4 miles and make a left on Bear Creek Road (paved County Road 18). Continue 9.6 miles; make a right on gravel Forest Road 36. Go another 8.7 miles to Forest Road 3650 where you'll make another right. The trailhead is off Road 3650, .3 mile ahead.

The hike: Arch Rock is a perfect family hike. It's short, yet scenic. Located in the Blue Mountains, Arch Rock is but one basis for hiking this trail. You may also see woodpeckers, mule deer, and on occasion, coyotes. In addition, you'll see pack rat nests beneath overhanging boulders and in various rock shelters.

Begin hiking Arch Rock Trail, climbing moderately and crossing intermittently between open slopes and through the trees. Also you'll hike among various rock formations before reaching Arch Rock at .3 mile.

One note of warning. The Forest Service reports that "it is quite dangerous to stand directly beneath the arch." Various forms of erosion—gravity, freezing, thawing, etc.—result in rockfall. Be careful!

HIKE 45 *CEDAR GROVE BOTANICAL AREA*

General description: A short day hike in the Malheur National Forest.
General location: About forty miles west of John Day and eighty-two miles east of Prineville.
Maps: Aldrich Mountain 15-minute USGS quad.
Difficulty: Moderate.
Length: About one mile one way.
Elevations: 5,895 to 5,300 feet.
Special attractions: Solitude, grove of cedar trees, wildflowers.
Water availability: Buck Cabin Creek.
Best season: Late May through October.
For more information: Bear Valley Ranger District, 528 Main St., John Day, OR 97845; (541) 575-2110.
Permit: None.
Finding the trailhead From Dayville (cafe, market, gas), go east on U.S. 26 for 13.1 miles; make a right on paved Forest Road 21. If traveling west from Mt. Vernon (all services), drive 9.9 miles on U.S. 26 to the same junction. Pass the Billy Fields Campground, a free camp at 6.5 miles. Piped water isn't available, but there are picnic tables, fire pits, outhouses. Sites are shady and situated along Fields Creek.

Continue up Forest Road 21 for another 3.4 miles; make a right on Forest Road 2150, a gravel road. Take this for 5.9 miles to the signed trailhead.

The hike: This trail leads to a unique area where Alaska cedar trees grow, the only such place within several hundred miles. Open to hikers, the trail leads down the slope to the Cedar Grove Botanical Area.

Begin hiking the Cedar Grove National Recreation Trail which leads through the trees. The grade is easy for the first .2 mile where you'll enter the fenced botanical area. From here it's a moderate (sometimes steep) descent.

Along the way, there's a good view of Fields Peak and the valley below

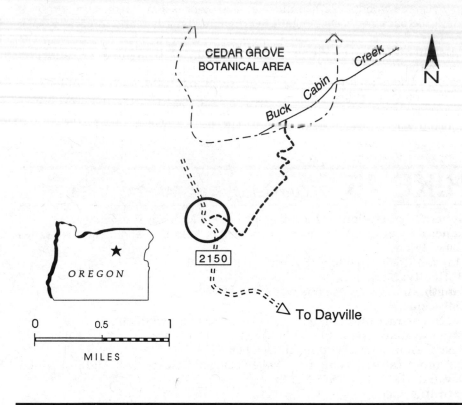

at .6 mile. Continue down to a creek at .8 mile. Just prior you'll pass a trail on the right. The trail straight ahead loops around and back to this point at one mile. This completes the loop.

Vegetation is lush along the hike with lupines, vanilla leaf, and wild roses commonly seen. Also there are huckleberries.

Twin Pillars Trail.

HIKE 46 *TWIN PILLARS*

General description: A round-trip day hike in the Mill Creek Wilderness.
General location: Approximately twenty miles northeast of Prineville.
Maps: Ochoco Reservoir 7.5-minute USGS quad.
Difficulty: Moderate.
Length: About 5.3 miles.
Elevations: 3,700 to 5,100 feet.
Special attractions: Old-growth ponderosa pine, solitude, wildlife, close-up

view of Twin Pillars, a unique rock formation.

Water availability: Mill Creek.

Best season: May through October. (Mill Creek Road is plowed during the winter for year-round access.)

For more information: Prineville Ranger District,3160 N.E. Third St., P.O. Box 490, Prineville, OR 97754; (541) 447-9641.

Permit: None.

Finding the trailhead: Reach the trailhead by driving east from Prineville on U.S. Highway 26 for 10.2 miles. Go north on Mill Creek Road for 10.8 miles to the Wildcat Campground. (Mill Creek Road becomes Forest Road 33 before reaching the campground.)

HIKE 46 *TWIN PILLARS*

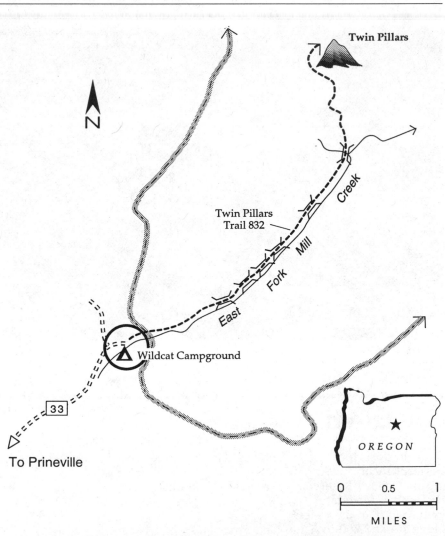

The hike: Signed Twin Pillars Trail 832 (a designated national recreation trail) follows along the edge of East Fork Mill Creek then crosses over the road and heads back into the trees before reaching the wilderness boundary at .2 mile.

You'll have to ford the creek several times as you ascend through old growth ponderosa, a carpet of grasses and wildflowers decorating the forest floor in May and June. Ahead there are numerous bridge crossings over the creek.

Along the way you might see pileated woodpeckers, goshawks, and wild turkeys, three of the many species of birds inhabiting the wilderness. Introduced to the 17,400-acre preserve several years ago, the wild turkeys are thought to be "doing fair."

At just over five miles Twin Pillars looms nearby. You'll see a sign pointing to the unique rock formation.

HIKE 47 *BLUE BASIN OVERLOOK TRAIL*

General description: A short loop day hike in Fossil Beds National Monument.
General location: About forty miles west of John Day and eighty-two miles east of Prineville.
Maps: Mt. Misery 7.5-minute USGS quad.
Difficulty: Moderate.
Length: About 3.4 miles.
Elevations: 2,150 to 2,800 feet.
Special attractions: Great views of Blue Basin and areas surrounding John Day Fossil Beds National Monument.
Water availability: None.
Best season: Year-round, but may be impassable during wet weather.
For more information: John Day Fossil Beds National Monument, HCR 82, Box 126, Kimberly, OR 97848; (541) 987-2333.
Permit: None. Please note, however, hikers must stay on the trail. Hiking off-trail is prohibited.
Finding the trailhead: The trail is located off Oregon 19, 14.4 miles south of Kimberly and 11.9 miles northwest of Dayville. Both towns have a market and gas; Dayville has a cafe. The visitors center for John Day Fossil Beds National Monument is 3.2 miles south of Blue Basin Trailhead.

The hike: This is one of those trails where you'll probably find yourself stopping a lot to view your magnificent surroundings. Although you can hike the trail in less than two hours, you may want to allow more time for just sitting and looking.

There's an outhouse at the Blue Basin trailhead where you'll find two trails to hike. Dogs are allowed on both trails as long as they are leashed.

Begin hiking the Blue Basin Overlook Trail by going left and climbing the easy then moderate grade, up a drainage that narrows as you climb. Watch for coyotes, chukars and badgers along the way. Be sure to keep looking back to the west as the views are tremendous.

Begin hiking some steep switchbacks at 1.2 miles. At 1.4 miles you'll find a lone juniper tree with a bench for resting and enjoying the view. Trees are

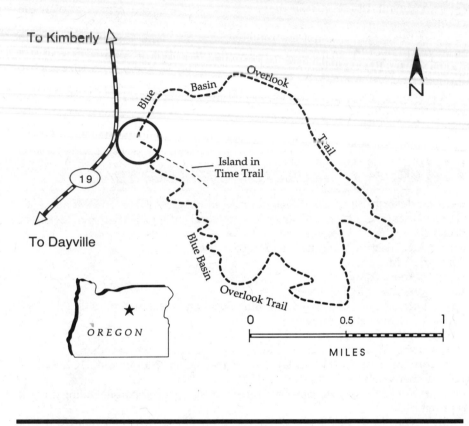

To Kimberly

Blue Basin Overlook

Trail

Island in
Time Trail

19

To Dayville

Blue Basin

Overlook Trail

OREGON

```
0                    0.5                    1

MILES
```

few and far between in this country, so you'll want to take advantage of the shade on hot days.

Reach the top of a ridge and a fork at 1.7 miles. A view trail takes off for 200 yards to the right. There's a another bench here and an excellent view into the Blue Basin amphitheater.

Back on the trail begin an easy descent, with the only ups while crossing gullies. Enter private land by climbing up and over a ladder which straddles a fence at 1.8 miles. Exit private property the same way at 2.2 miles. There are wonderful views as you circle the basin.

At 2.6 miles begin a steep descent via switchbacks. This trail merges with the Islands in Time Trail at 3.2 miles. Head left, reaching the trailhead in another .2 mile.

If you'd like to hike the Island in Time Trail, go right another .4 mile. This trail follows a narrow watercourse into Blue Basin, a natural amphitheater carved out of the green volcanic ash of the John Day formation. Many fossils

Donna Ikenberry hiking the Carroll Rim Trail; Painted Hills in the background.

have been discovered in this and surrounding areas. You'll find replicas of some of the fossils along this interpretative trail. Please note, volcanic ash is slippery when wet. One note of caution: although uncommon, rattlesnakes do live in the area.

HIKE 48 *CARROLL RIM*

General description: A short day hike in John Day Fossil Beds National Monument.

General location: About seventy-seven miles west of John Day and forty miles east of Prineville.

Maps: Painted Hills 7.5-minute USGS quad.

Difficulty: Moderate.

Length: About .7 mile one way.

Elevations: 2,060 to 2,440 feet.

Special attractions: Great views of the Painted Hills unit of John Day Fossil Beds National Monument and surrounding areas.

Water availability: None.

Best season: Year-round, but may be impassable during wet weather.

For more information: John Day Fossil Beds National Monument, HCR 82, Box 126, Kimberly, OR 97848; (541) 987-2333.

Permit: None, however monument personnel ask that you please stay on the trail.

Finding the trailhead: From Mitchell, a tiny town offering a motel, cafes, markets and gas, go west on U.S. 26 for 3.5 miles. At this point you'll head right (north) on a paved road where a sign points the way to the Painted Hills unit of the John Day Fossil Beds National Monument. Drive 5.6 miles and make a left, again following the signs. The road turns to gravel as you reach a fork in .3 mile. To the left there are restrooms, water and picnic tables. This is a day use area only as camping is not allowed on monument grounds. Go right .8 mile to the trailhead. Parking is on the left.

The hike: For a spectacular view of the Painted Hills, climb this moderate trail to the top of Carroll Rim. From here you'll look down upon multi-colored hills and nearby Sutton Mountain. In case you were wondering, these cliffs are comprised of John Day ignimbrite. "Formed as a fiery cloud of volcanic ash," according to one monument leaflet, "the ignimbrite solidified as the hot ash particles welded themselves together, resulting in the rimrock we see today."

Although the trailhead parking area sees some traffic, most people decide

HIKE 48 *CARROLL RIM*

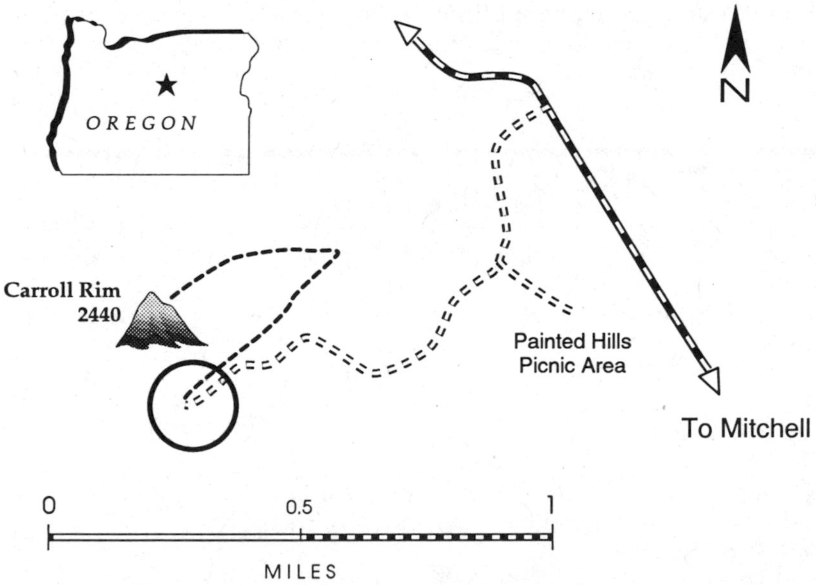

OREGON

Carroll Rim
2440

Painted Hills
Picnic Area

To Mitchell

N

0   0.5   1

MILES

not to hike the trail for some reason. I hiked Carroll Rim on a nice August day and enjoyed the view alone. Signing the register, I counted only five other hikers in the ten days preceding my hike.

Climb the moderate grade up the open rocky slope, climbing a giant switchback that traverses both the south and north sides of the rim. At .7 mile reach the top of the rim and a wonderful 360-degree view down upon the marshmallow-like Painted Hills and beyond.

HIKE 49 *DIAMOND PEAK LOOP*

General description: A three- to four-day round-trip backpack in the Diamond Peak Wilderness.
General location: About thirty miles southeast of Oakridge.
Maps: Willamette Pass 7.5-minute, Diamond Peak 7.5-minute USGS quads; Diamond Peak Wilderness map.
Difficulty: Moderate.
Length: About twenty-three miles.
Elevations: 4,800 to 7,040 feet.
Special attractions: Picturesque lakes, fantastic views.
Water availability: See description.
Best season: July through October, although the wilderness is popular in winter as well.
For more information: Crescent Ranger District, P.O. Box 208, Crescent, OR 97733; (541) 433-2234 or Rigdon Ranger District, 44098 Salmon Creek Rd., Oakridge, OR 97463; (541) 782-2283.
Permit: Permits are necessary and available from both the Willamette and Deschutes National Forests. The permits are free of charge.
Finding the trailhead: Begin the loop at the West Odell Campground, at Odell Lake. The campground is twenty-eight miles southeast of Oakridge, via Oregon 58. Turn right at the signed junction, descending Forest Road 5810 (Odell Lake Road) for 1.8 miles to the Mount Yoran Lake trailhead.

The hike: Diamond Peak rises 8,744 feet above the surrounding wilderness for which it was named, a preserve decorated with glacier-formed lakes, dancing wildflowers, and a wealth of wildlife.

Hike Mount Yoran Trail 49, crossing some railroad tracks, then reaching a junction at .2 mile. Head left on Whitefish Creek Trail 42, hiking to Diamond View Lake at five miles.

Pass several ponds en route to a junction at 5.8 miles. Go right on Crater Butte Trail 44, following a creek as you make your way past Snell and Mountain View lakes. Just past the ten-mile mark you'll come to a sign. Head to the right, hiking an old road to the PCT junction at 10.5 miles. Make another right, now hiking the PCT.

Cross another stream as you climb to 11.7 miles where there is a good view to the south. This is also a popular exit point for those hiking the south spur to the top of Diamond Peak.

The 52,329-acre wilderness is popular with mountain climbers who bag three popular summits—Diamond Peak, Mt. Yoran, and Lakeview Mountain.

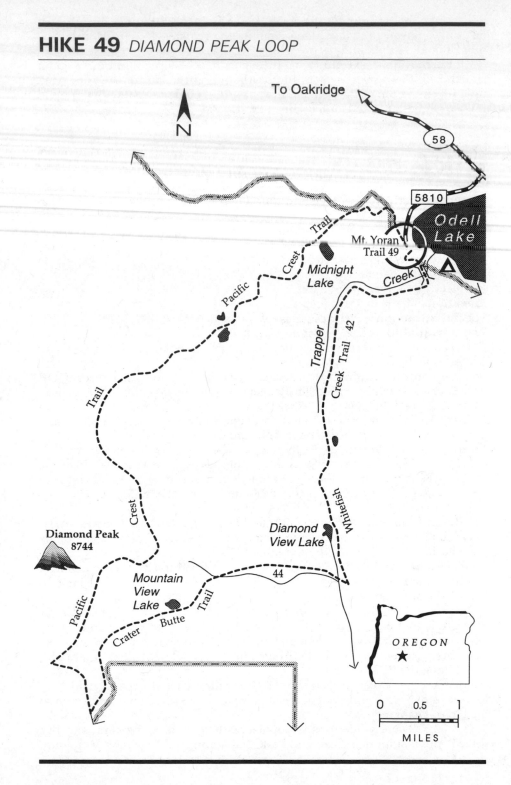

To Oakridge

N

58

5810

Odell Lake

Mt. Yoran
Trail 49

Midnight Lake

Crest Trail

Creek

Pacific

Trapper

Creek Trail 42

Trail

Whitefish

Crest

Diamond Peak
8744

Diamond View Lake

Pacific

Mountain View Lake

Trail

44

Crater Butte

OREGON

0   0.5   1

MILES

Seasonal ponds/Diamond Peak as seen from the PCT.

Diamond Peak is a relatively easy summit to climb, while the latter two offer a challenge to skilled mountaineers.

Again there are more stream crossings as you hike across the open slope then descend through the trees past numerous lakes and ponds to a junction at 22.5 miles. Exit the wilderness, turning left on an old road for 200 feet, then go right and cross some railroad tracks in .5 mile. Continue 100 yards to Odell Lake Road. Make a right, reaching the trailhead in another .3 mile.

HIKE 50 *WALDO MOUNTAIN*

General description: A round-trip day hike in the Waldo Lake Wilderness.
General location: Approximately twenty-one miles east of Oakridge.
Maps: Waldo Mountain 7.5-minute, Blair Lake 7.5-minute USGS quads; Waldo Lake Wilderness map.
Difficulty: Moderate.
Length: About 3.1 miles one way.
Elevations: 4,400 to 6,357 feet.
Special attractions: Rhododendrons, Washington lilies, and terrific views.
Water availability: None.
Best season: July through October.
For more information: Oakridge Ranger District, 46375 Highway 58, Westfir, OR 97492; (541) 782-2291.
Permit: Registration box at the trailhead.
Finding the trailhead: Reach the trailhead from Oakridge, by turning north off Oregon 58 at the only stop light in town. Turn right shortly thereafter, following the sign to Salmon Creek Road (Road 24). Continue to Forest Road 2417 at 11.3 miles. Turn left, driving another 6.2 miles to Forest Road 2424. Make a right, reaching the trailhead in 3.8 miles.

Waldo Mountain Lookout.

HIKE 50 *WALDO MOUNTAIN*

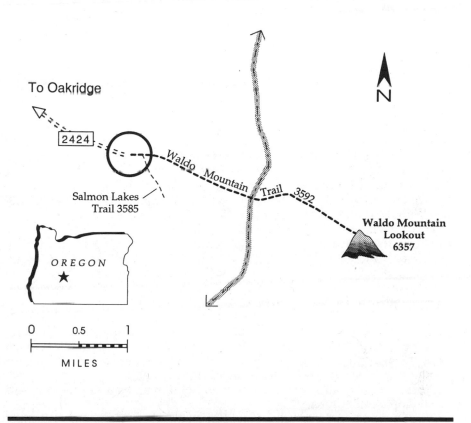

The hike: Begin hiking the Salmon Lakes Trail 3585, passing into the wilderness in 200 feet. (Waldo Lake Wilderness map shows the wilderness boundary about a mile or so down the trail.) You'll come to a fork another 100 feet or so down the trail. Head left, hiking Waldo Mountain Trail 3592. The trail passes through thick forest and rich vegetation where bear grass, rhododendrons and lilies are common. Peak season for rhododendrons is sometime between mid-June and mid-July.

Reach another junction at 2.1 miles. Head left, continuing on the Waldo Mountain Trail. You'll reach the summit and a lookout in another mile.

The lookout is manned from July 1 to September 1. A volunteer lives and works in the lookout, keeping a sharp eye out for fires. From the 6,357-foot peak there are views of Mounts Hood and Jefferson, the Three Sisters, and many other Cascade peaks.

Also, you'll see Waldo Lake, one of the world's purest lakes and the lake for which the wilderness was named although the lake rests just outside the wilderness boundary. Spanning more than ten square miles, it is Oregon's second largest lake (Upper Klamath is the largest) and at 420 feet deep, it's the second deepest lake in the Beaver State as well. Crater Lake dips down to 1,932 feet.

HIKE 51 *LILLIAN FALLS*

General description: A short round-trip day hike in the 37,162-acre Waldo Lake Wilderness.
General location: About twenty-two miles east of Oakridge.
Maps: Waldo Lake 7.5-minute USGS quad; Waldo Lake Wilderness map.
Difficulty: Moderate.
Length: About 1.2 miles one way.
Elevations: 3,400 to 4,000 feet.
Special attractions: Mature forest, waterfall.
Water availability: See description.
Best season: May through November.
For more information: Oakridge Ranger District, 46375 Highway 58, Westfir, OR 97492; (541) 782-2291.
Permit: Registration box just past the trailhead.
Finding the trailhead: Reach the trailhead by driving to downtown Oakridge, off Oregon 58. At the town's only stop light, go north then right, following the sign to Salmon Creek Road (which later becomes Forest Road 24). Travel 14.3 miles on Road 24 then make a left on Forest Road 2421, going another 8.8 miles to the Black Creek Trailhead.

The hike: Hike Black Creek Trail 3551, passing a multitude of berry bushes en route to Edith Creek and the wilderness boundary at .1 mile. Hike through dense Douglas-fir, western red cedar, and mountain hemlock, watching for maiden hair ferns which border some of the streams.

Cross several small streams before reaching Lillian Falls, a gorgeous falls located on Nettie Creek.

Those wishing to visit Waldo Lake can continue on the trail to Klovdahl Bay, another 2.6 miles away.

HIKE 51 *LILLIAN FALLS*

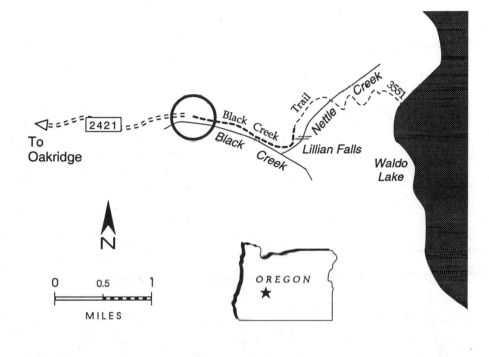

HIKE 52 *NORTH FORK WILLAMETTE RIVER*

General description: A short round-trip day hike into the Waldo Lake Wilderness.

General location: Approximately thirty miles northeast of Oakridge.

Maps: Waldo Mountain 7.5-minute USGS quad; Waldo Lake Wilderness map.

Difficulty: Easy.

Length: About 2.5 miles one way.

Elevations: 3,000 to 3,100 feet.

Special attractions: Old-growth forest, ancient cedar trees, wildlife.

Water availability: In addition to the river, there are many streams.

Best season: April through November.

For more information: Oakridge Ranger District, 46375 Highway 58, Westfir, OR 97492; (541) 782-2291.

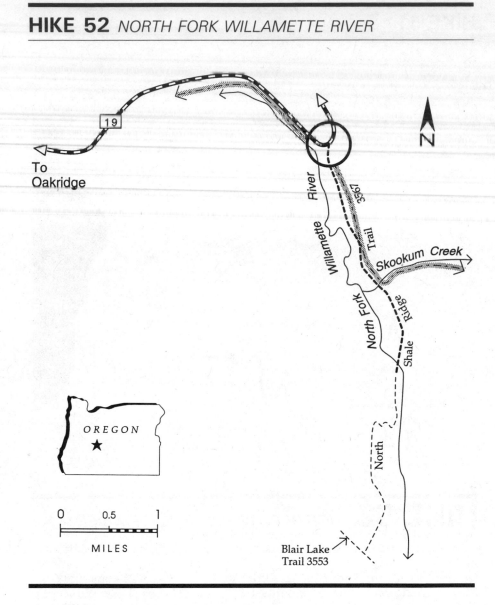

To
Oakridge

19

Willamette River

3567

Trail

North Fork

Skookum Creek

Shale Ridge

North

OREGON
★

0   0.5   1

MILES

Blair Lake
Trail 3553

Permit: Registration box at the trailhead.
Finding the trailhead: Located on the western slopes of the Oregon Cascades,
the trailhead is reached by driving from Westfir, a tiny town located just north
of Oakridge off Oregon 58. From Westfir travel north on North Fork Road
19 for thirty miles. You'll see the signed trailhead on your right.

The hike: This is a perfect trail for families as the trail is flat and easy to
hike. Hike Shale Ridge Trail 3567, following an old road which now serves
as a trail and leads to a standard trail farther along. Enter the wilderness in
100 yards.

In less than two miles you'll enter a grove of ancient cedar trees. Some of the aged western red cedars seen today are more than 800 years old. Northwest Coast Indians used trees like these for totem poles, lodges, and canoes. In fact, the trees were also known as "canoe-cedar." Native Americans made special war canoes by hollowing out the massive cedar trunks. They also used cedar for boxes, helmets, batons, and many other items. Modern man found many uses as well; items include fenceposts, utility poles, roof shingles, and boats.

At about the 2.5-mile mark you'll reach the North Fork Willamette River. Although the prettiest part of the trail ends here, the trail does not. It merges with the Blair Lake Trail in another 3.8 miles. To continue the hike, ford the river (crossing can be dangerous at times) and ascend the steep trail to Shale Ridge. The trail is a bit difficult to follow at times, but red ribbons mark the way.

Willamette River.

HIKE 53 *OLALLIE MOUNTAIN*

General description: A round-trip day hike in the Three Sisters Wilderness.

General location: Approximately fifty-five miles east of Eugene.

Maps: French Mountain 7.5-minute USGS quad; Three Sisters Wilderness map.

Difficulty: Moderate.

Length: About 3.6 miles one way.

Elevations: 4,240 to 5,708 feet

Special attractions: Great views, wonderful wildflower displays.

Water availability: See description.

Best season: June through October.

For more information: Blue River Ranger District, Off-State Highway 126, Blue River, OR 97413; (541) 822-3317.

Permit: Permits are necessary in the summer. Contact the Deschutes or Willamette National Forests for more information regarding the free permits in this, the busiest of Oregon's wilderness areas.

Finding the trailhead: Reach the trailhead via Oregon Highway 126, located four miles east of the small town of Blue River. Make a right on Forest Road 19 and go 3.3 miles to a junction. Head left on Forest Road 1993 for 14.1 miles to the trailhead.

The hike: If you like terrific views and lots of wildflowers, then Olallie Mountain is the place to be.

Hike the Olallie Trail through the forest, entering the wilderness in .1 mile. Cross two small streams at .6 and 1.8 miles. Both streams normally flow year-round, but occasionally they dry up so you'll want to carry water.

Reach the Olallie Mountain Trail at 2.2 miles. Make a right, passing through Olallie Meadow en route to the summit. There's an unmanned lookout on top. Built in the 1930s, it is open only during the summer months.

From the summit, you'll see much of the 280,500-acre preserve. In the distance, you'll see from Diamond Peak in the south to Mt. Hood in the north.

HIKE 53 *OLALLIE MOUNTAIN*

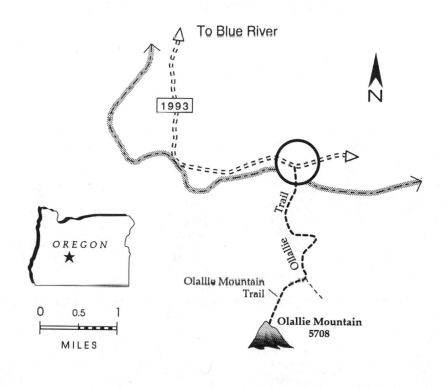

To Blue River

1993

N

OREGON

0   0.5   1
MILES

Trail

Olallie

Olallie Mountain
Trail

Olallie Mountain
5708

HIKE 54 *SOUTH SISTER*

General description: A long round-trip day hike in the Three Sisters Wilderness. A backpack trip using Moraine Lake as a base camp is also a popular choice.

General location: About twenty-seven miles west of Bend.

Maps: Broken Top 7.5-minute, South Sister 7.5-minute USGS quads; Three Sisters Wilderness map.

Difficulty: Difficult.

Length: About 6.7 miles one way.

Elevations: 5,450 to 10,358 feet.

Special attractions: Outstanding views from atop Oregon's third highest peak.

Water availability: See description.

Best season: July through October.

For more information: Bend Ranger District, 1230 NE 3rd, Bend, OR 97701; (541) 388-5664.

Permit: Permits are necessary although free of charge. Contact the Deschutes or Willamette National Forests for more information.

Finding the trailhead: Reach the Green Lakes Trailhead by driving west from Bend via the Cascades Lakes Highway (Oregon 46) for twenty-seven miles. You'll see the large trailhead across the road from Sparks Lake.

The hike: Although Moraine Lake is a popular base camp for those aiming for the top of South Sister, I would recommend a long day hike. The lake gets crowded at times, especially on weekends and holidays, and the less impact on the land the better.

HIKE 54 *SOUTH SISTER*

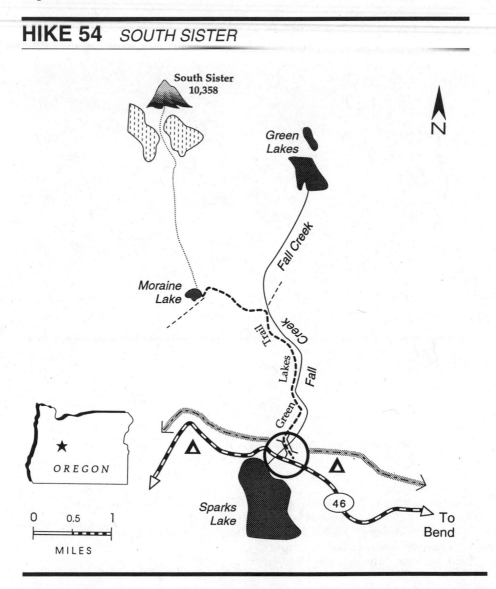

Camp at Moraine Lake.

Hike the Green Lakes Trail, passing into the wilderness in about 100 yards. Ascend along Fall Creek until reaching a junction at 2.2 miles; make a left and continue until you reach Moraine Lake at 3.3 miles. There's a terrific view of South Sister from the twelve-acre lake. Also you'll see a spur trail leading nearly 4,000 feet up to the summit.

Unlike several other routes which lead to the summit, the route from Moraine Lake is not a technical climb, just a long, steep hike up the mountain. Hikers attempting this climb should remember, though, that this is a 10,000-foot mountain, subject to quick and sometimes violent weather changes and pack accordingly.

You'll see several unmaintained trails leading north from Moraine lake. Choose one and hike out of the flat basin where you'll begin climbing rapidly.

Although you will be traveling cross-country, it's quite easy to see where other hikers have walked.

You'll reach the south end of Lewis Glacier at 5.3 miles. Head left and up the cinder-covered slopes, climbing the loose scree to the south end of the crater rim at 6.4 miles. Hike the rim to the true summit while drinking in the view and standing in awe of the aqua-blue water that fills the summit crater most of the year. Snow will cover much of the route early in the summer, so an ice-axe and knowledge of its use is recommended.

You'll see much of Oregon from the summit, including the other Sisters, North (10,094 feet) and Middle (10,053 feet). Once called Faith, Hope and Charity by pioneer missionaries, these three lofty peaks dominate the 280,500-acre preserve and the surrounding region.

HIKE 55 BIG LAKE TO McKENZIE PASS

General description: A one-way day hike (with shuttle) or a three-day round-trip backpack in the Mt. Washington Wilderness.
General location: About forty miles northwest of Bend.
Maps: Mt. Washington 7.5-minute USGS quad; Mt. Washington Wilderness map.
Difficulty: Moderate to difficult.
Length: Approximately thirteen miles one way.
Elevations: 4,644 to 6,305 feet.
Special attractions: Immense lava flows, wonderful views, abundant wildlife, wildflowers.
Water availability: Big Lake Campground.
Best season: July through October.
For more information: McKenzie Ranger District, State Highway 126, McKenzie Bridge, OR 97413; (541) 822-3381 or Sisters Ranger District, P.O. Box 249, Sisters, OR 97759; (541) 549-2111.
Permit: None.
Finding the trailhead: Reach Big Lake by traveling U.S. Highway 20 to Big Lake Road (Forest Road 2690), located twenty-one miles west of Sisters. Go south for 3.2 miles, then left on Forest Road 811 for .5 mile to the signed trailhead. (To reach Big Lake do not turn onto Road 811. Continue .2 mile further on Road 2690. A trail leads from the lake to the PCT.)

Reach the McKenzie Pass PCT trailhead by driving Oregon 242. This road is closed during the winter months so you'll want to c heck with the Forest Service for opening dates. It usually opens sometime around June or July. The trailhead is fifteen miles west of Sisters, twenty-six miles east of McKenzie Bridge.

The hike: About thirteen miles of the Pacific Crest Trail (PCT), a 2,400-mile Mexico-to-Canada trail, weaves through the Mt. Washington Wilderness, a land of vast lava flows, stunted trees, forest and meadow.

The PCT is a perfect hike for those with a shuttle available. If you begin at the south end (McKenzie Pass) and have a shuttle waiting at the north end (Big Lake), you'll save yourself about 600 feet of climbing. We opted to begin in the north, however, as those in need of a shuttle can rarely be choosy.

HIKE 55 *BIG LAKE TO McKENZIE PASS*

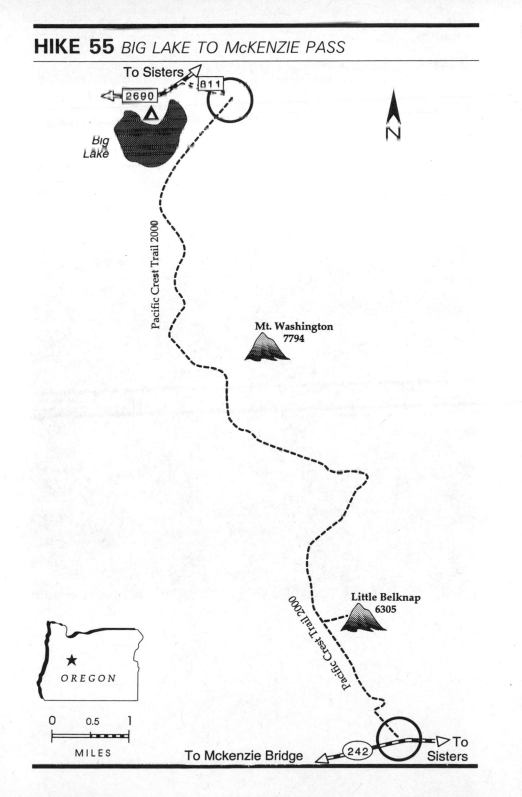

To Sisters

2690

811

Big Lake

N

Pacific Crest Trail 2000

Mt. Washington
7794

Little Belknap
6305

Pacific Crest Trail 2000

OREGON

0   0.5   1

MILES

To Mckenzie Bridge

242

To Sisters

From the trailhead near Big Lake, go south on the PCT. A sign claims this is Trail 2007 when it is actually Trail 2000. Enter the wilderness in seventy-five yards.

You'll travel through a forest of lodgepole pine, hemlock and white pine en route to a junction at two miles. The spur trail leads to Big Lake, .2 mile away. There's another trail junction marked with a rock cairn and orange flag at 2.9 miles. This unmaintained trail leads to Mt. Washington, which is a technical climb and should not be attempted unless you have the proper gear and experience. The rock on the mountain crumbles away very easily.

Climb through meadows and along semi-open slopes as you hike south past Mt. Washington, hiking a lava-strewn trail for about the last three to four miles of the hike.

Reach the Little Belknap Crater junction at 10.6 miles. There's a .2 mile trail leading to a 360-degree view of the surrounding area. It is a must-see.

View from Scott Mountain. Hayrick Butte, Three Fingered Jack, Mt. Jefferson and Mt. Hood in background.

HIKE 56 *SCOTT MOUNTAIN*

General description: A round-trip day hike in the Mt. Washington Wilderness.

General location: Approximately twenty-two miles east of McKenzie Bridge.

Maps: Linton Lake 7.5-minute USGS quad; Mt. Washington Wilderness map.

Difficulty: Moderate to difficult.

Length: About four miles one way.

Elevations: 4,800 to 6,116 feet.

Special attractions: Excellent views, good fishing.

Water availability: See description.

Best season: July through October.

For more information: McKenzie Ranger District, McKenzie Bridge, OR 97413; (541) 822-3381.

Permit: None.

Finding the trailhead: From the small town of McKenzie Bridge, travel east on Oregon 126. Reach the junction of Oregon 242 at 4.8 miles. Turn right on Oregon 242, which is closed during the winter. Check with the Forest Service for opening dates. It usually opens in June or July. Drive 15.9 miles to Forest Road 260; make a left, going .9 mile to the trailhead at Scott Lake.

The hike: From atop Scott Mountain you'll get a good look at the Mt. Washington Wilderness, a land wrought with massive lava flows. In fact, so much of the preserve is covered by lava (about seventy-five square miles) that it is often called the "Black Wilderness."

Begin hiking Benson Trail 3502, traveling through the forest where huckleberry bushes abound. Cross a small creek and continue to Benson Lake and the wilderness boundary in 1.3 miles. Pass a series of ponds as you head to a spur trail leading to Tenas Lakes at 2.5 miles. A short trail (.1 mile) leads to the largest of seven rock-lined lakes.

You'll come to an unsigned junction near 3.7 miles. Head up to the left, climbing the steep grade to the summit where you'll see Oregon's five highest peaks: Mt. Jefferson, Mt. Hood, and the Three—North, Middle and South—Sisters.

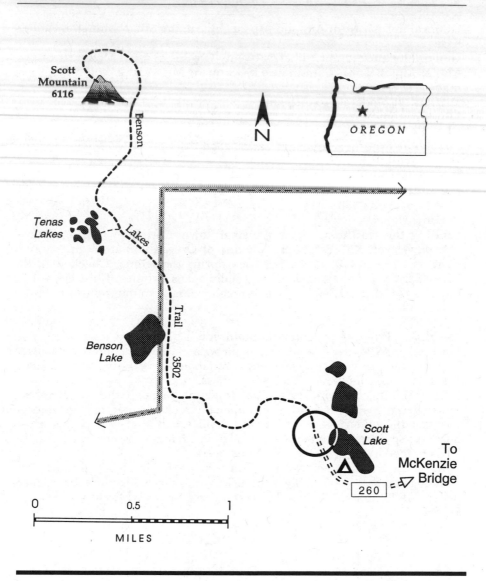

Cathedral Rocks.

HIKE 57 *CATHEDRAL ROCKS*

General description: A long round-trip day hike or a two-day round-trip backpack in the Mt. Jefferson Wilderness.

General location: Approximately seventy miles southeast of Salem.

Maps: Marion Lake 7.5-minute, Mount Jefferson 7.5-minute USGS quads; Mt. Jefferson Wilderness map.

Difficulty: Moderate to difficult.

Length: About 7.8 miles one way.

Elevations: 4,160 to 6,000 feet.

Special attractions: Fine views, solitude (along portions of the trail), wildflowers.

Water availability: See description.

Best season: July through October.

For more information: Detroit Ranger District, Highway 20, Box 320, Mill City, OR 97360; (541) 854-3366.

Permit: Free permits are necessary in the summer. Contact either the Deschutes or the Willamette national forests for more information.

Finding the trailhead: Travel Oregon 22 from Idanha, a tiny town, for 10.5 miles; make a left (head east) on Forest Road 2253, driving 5.5 miles to the trailhead.

The hike: A potpourri of pleasure, Mt. Jefferson is one of the largest and most popular wilderness areas in Oregon. Its 111,177 acres consists of dense forests, alpine meadows where fragile wildflowers dance a windy tune, and swift rivers. There are tiny streams, lava fields, open ridges, and mountains to climb.

Bingham Ridge Trail 3421 begins in an old clearcut, but enters the forest and wilderness in .4 mile. The trail ends at a junction in another three miles. Lake of the Woods Trail 3493 runs to the left and right. Go left to 4.6 miles and an unnamed lake where birders should look for flickers, grouse, and other species. Mt. Jefferson is visible from here.

Pass Papoose Lake and a small pond before reaching a junction at 5.9 miles. Head right on Trail 3440 (a sign points the way to the PCT), crossing a couple of huge rock slides where pikas whistle a warning.

Farther along you'll look 800 feet below to Hunts Cove, a lush basin of lakes and streams. Cathedral Rocks is visible to the east. For a closer view hike to 7.8 miles and the PCT junction. From here, stunted hemlock and dainty wildflowers adorn lava slopes, a fitting foreground for the rugged Cathedral Rocks and Mt. Jefferson seen behind.

HIKE 57 *CATHEDRAL ROCKS*

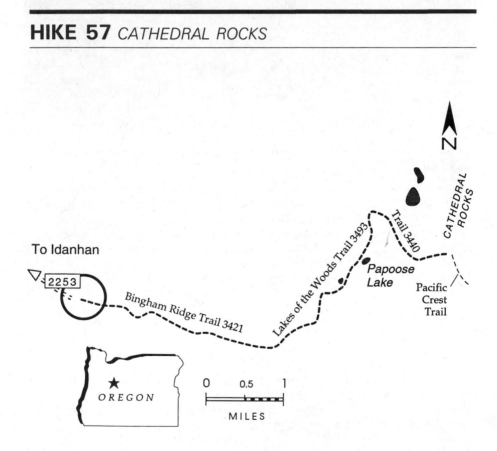

Egg Creek.

HIKE 58 *CHIMNEY PEAK*

General description: A very long round-trip day hike or a two- to three-day round-trip backpack in the Middle Santiam Wilderness.
General location: Roughly sixty-five miles southeast of Albany.
Maps: Chimney Peak 7.5-minute USGS quad.
Difficulty: Moderate to difficult.
Length: About nine miles one way.
Elevations: 2,300 to 4,965 feet.
Special attractions: Solitude, lush vegetation, old-growth forest, wildflowers.
Water availability: See description.
Best season: June through October.
For more information: Sweet Home Ranger District, 3225 Highway 20, Sweet Home, OR 97386; (541) 367-5168.
Permit: None.
Finding the trailhead: From Sweet Home, a small town about twenty-five miles southeast of Albany, go east on U.S. Highway 20. After twenty-five miles turn left at Upper Soda (which consists of a restaurant), traveling Forest Road 2041 (Soda Fork Road). Reach the trailhead in 16.9 miles.

The hike: Stretching from east to west, the Chimney Peak Trail—the only major trail in the preserve—spans the Middle Santiam Wilderness, offering solitude to those who hike here.

Hike signed Chimney Peak Trail 3382, entering the 8,542-acre wilderness in fifty feet. Pass old-growth western red cedar as you make your way past several creeks while en route to a clearcut at 1.2 miles. In case you were wondering, this area is out of the wilderness.

Proceed back into the wilderness in .2 mile. Cross Swamp Creek before reaching Donaca Lake at 2.8 miles. The trail heads up and around the northwest end of lake then crosses Egg Creek at 4.3 miles, Fitt Creek at 5.7, and several more small streams before reaching the last stream at 7.2 miles. Please note, some of the creeks dry up early in the season.

Around the eight-mile mark the trail steepens, climbing over 600 feet in elevation in less than a mile. Old stairs lead towards the summit. Although the Forest Service doesn't recommend climbing them, you may feel secure in doing so. Climb at your own discretion. The stairs and steep trail lead to the site of an old lookout. Views from the summit are spectacular.

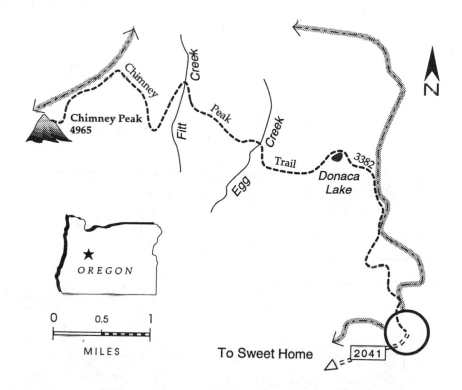

Chimney Creek

Fitt Creek

Chimney Peak
4965

Peak

Egg Creek

Trail

3382

Donaca Lake

OREGON

0   0.5   1

MILES

To Sweet Home

2041

N

HIKE 59 *BULL OF THE WOODS LOOP*

General description: A three-day loop backpack in the Bull of the Woods Wilderness.

General location: Nearly seventy miles southeast of Portland.

Maps: Mother Lode Mtn. 7.5-minute, Bull of the Woods 7.5-minute USGS quads; Bull of the Woods Wilderness map.

Difficulty: Difficult.

Length: About nineteen miles.

Elevations: 2,500 to 5,523 feet.

Special attractions: A waterfall, scenic Elk Lake Creek, old-growth forest, wildlife, and grand views.

Water availability: See description.

Best season: Mid-June through October.

For more information: Estacada Ranger District, 595 NW Industrial Way, Estacada, OR 97023; (503) 630-6861.

Permit: None.

Finding the trailhead: Reach the trailhead by driving to Detroit, a small town off Oregon 22, on the north shore of Detroit Lake. From town, head northeast on Forest Road 46; after 4.3 miles turn left on Forest Road 4697. Travel 2.2 miles and turn right on Forest Road 4698 which later turns to Forest Road 6370. Drive 18.9 miles to a junction; make a left (hairpin turn) on Forest Road 6380. Go 2.8 miles to the signed trail.

The hike: Although this hike is perfect for several days, it's a wonderful day hike as well—day hike, that is, if you limit yourself to the first five miles of the loop. So, if time is limited, try hiking the easiest five miles of them all.

Hike Elk Lake Trail 559, passing a waterfall and entering the wilderness in less than a mile. There are quite a few creek and stream crossings along the trail, all of which are done on foot. Use caution, especially when crossing Elk Lake Creek as it can be deep and swift.

HIKE 59 *BULL OF THE WOODS LOOP*

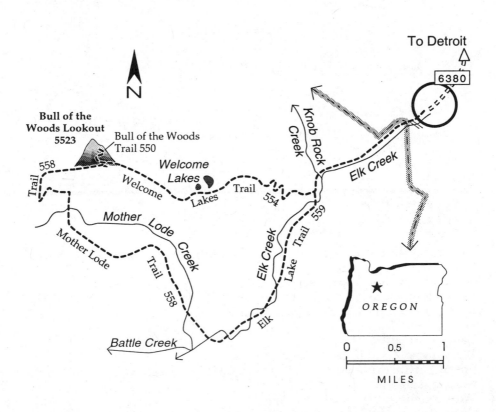

Reach a junction and the old Battle Ax Shelter at 5.1 miles. Built in the 1920s, the shelter buckled under heavy snow in 1988-89.

Head northwest on the Mother Lode Trail 558, crossing Battle Creek and Mother Lode Creek as you ascend the slope. There are some very steep sections along this portion of the trail.

You'll descend into the Mother Lode drainage then climb the steep grade through forest and semi-open slope to a junction at 11.2 miles. You'll cross a creek and your last chance for water for the time being at 9.6 miles.

Go north on the Bull of the Woods Trail 550, climbing to the lookout and a 360-degree view in .6 mile. Although manned during the summer, if you arrive before or after the fire spotter, you can stay in the shelter. The Forest Service asks, however, that you pack out all garbage and close all shutters when leaving. There is a pit toilet nearby.

Complete the loop by going back to the junction and turning left onto Welcome Lakes Trail 554. You'll reach the first of two lakes—Upper Welcome—at 14.1 miles. A creek and the spur trail leading to Lower Welcome is just up ahead.

Descend the moderate, sometimes steep grade, to Elk Creek Lake Trail at 16.7 miles. Go left to complete the loop.

HIKE 60 *TABLE ROCK*

General description: A short round-trip day hike in the Table Rock Wilderness.
General location: Forty air miles southeast of Portland.
Maps: Rooster Rock 7.5-minute USGS quad; Table Rock Wilderness map.
Difficulty: Moderate.
Length: About 2.5 miles one way.
Elevations: 3,760 to 4,881 feet.
Special attractions: Solitude, great views, basalt columns, wildflowers, wildlife.
Water availability: Stream near the trailhead.
Best season: Mid-June through October.
For more information: Bureau of Land Management, 1717 Fabry Road S.E., Salem, OR 97306; (503) 375-5646.
Permit: None.
Finding the trailhead: Reach the trailhead by driving to Molalla, a small town off Oregon 211. At the eastern edge of town you'll come to a fork; go right, traveling S. Mathias Road. Drive .3 mile before the road curves to the left and changes to S. Freyer Park Road. Go another 1.9 miles to a junction; head right on S. Dickey Prairie Road. Proceed 5.2 miles and cross the Molalla River where there is another name change—S. Molalla Road. Go 12.7 miles to the junction of Middle Fork and Copper Creek Roads. Make a left on Middle Fork Road and drive 2.6 miles to the Table Rock Access Road. Go right, driving another 6.6 miles to the signed trailhead.

The hike: The Table Rock Wilderness is different than most of Oregon's wilderness areas in that it is managed by the Bureau of Land Management (BLM).

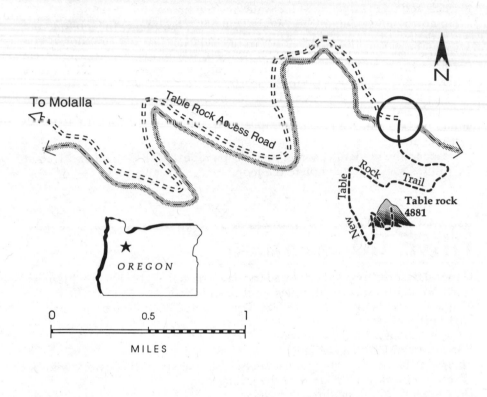

To Molalla

Table Rock Access Road

N

Table Rock Trail

Table rock
4881

New

Table

OREGON

★

0   0.5   1

MILES

All other wildernesses, with the exception of a portion of the Wild Rogue Wilderness, are managed by the Forest Service.

You'll enter the wilderness immediately upon hiking the New Table Rock Trail. Hike through dense forest decorated with lush understory (including rhododendrons which usually bloom in July) until reaching Table Rock's north face at 1.2 miles. From there you'll head up the semi-open west slope to a junction at 1.8 miles. Go to the left, traveling up the moderate to steep grade for a terrific view from atop Table Rock.

From the summit, three large Washington peaks are visible—Mount Rainier, Mt. St. Helens, and Mt. Adams. Oregon brags of it's five highest peaks, Mounts Hood, Jefferson and the Three Sisters.

HIKE 61 *HUCKLEBERRY MOUNTAIN*

General description: A long round-trip day hike in the Salmon-Huckleberry Wilderness.

General location: About fifty miles southeast of Portland.

Maps: Rhododendron 7.5-minute USGS quad; Salmon-Huckleberry Wilderness map.

Difficulty: Moderate to difficult.

Length: About 5.5 miles one way.

Elevations: 1,200 to 4,300 feet.

Special attractions: Outstanding views, wildflowers.

Water availability: Salmon River.

Best season: May through October.

For more information: Zigzag Ranger District, 70220 E. Highway 26, Zigzag, OR 97049; (503) 622-3191.

Permit: None.

Finding the trailhead: The trail begins at the Windowed Recreation Area, located off U.S. Highway 26, three miles west of Zigzag and fifteen miles east of Sandy.

The hike: There are wonderful views from atop Huckleberry Mountain, a long north-south ridge in the northwest corner of the Salmon-Huckleberry Wilderness.

Begin hiking signed Boulder Trail 783A, crossing the Salmon River in .1 mile. Hike level ground then begin climbing, entering the wilderness at 1.9 miles.

The Boulder Trail becomes the Plaza Trail 783 at 4.2 miles. Hike this past a myriad of colorful flowers in the proper season, including paintbrush, daisies, columbine, and foxglove. Although we were fogged in the day we hiked the trail, the Forest Service claims you can see several Washington peaks, including Mt. Rainier. Visible Oregon summits include Mt. Jefferson. The trail continues to the southern boundary of the 44,600-acre preserve at thirteen miles, but you'll reach the high point of the trail at about 5.5 miles.

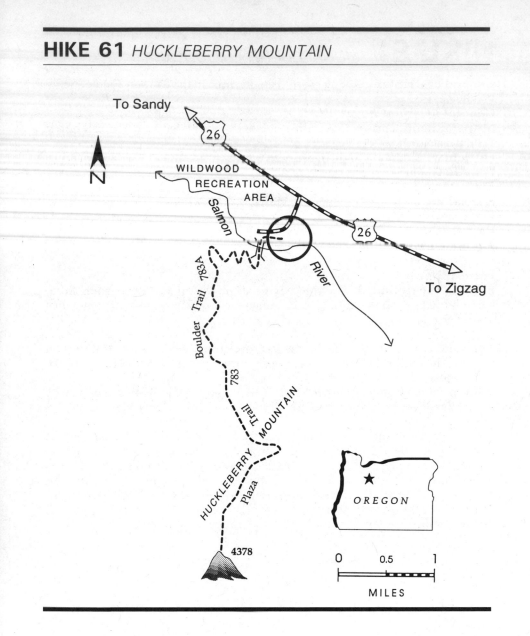

To Sandy

26

WILDWOOD
RECREATION
AREA

Salmon

26

River

To Zigzag

N

Boulder Trail 783A

783

Trail

HUCKLEBERRY MOUNTAIN

Plaza

4378

OREGON

0   0.5   1

MILES

HIKE 62 *SALMON RIVER*

General description: A two- to three-day round-trip backpack in the Salmon-Huckleberry Wilderness.

General location: Approximately fifty miles southeast of Portland.

Maps: Rhododendron 7.5-minute, High Rock 7.5-minute, Wolf Peak 7.5-minute USGS quads; Salmon-Huckleberry Wilderness map.

Difficulty: Moderate.

Length: About twelve miles one way.

Elevations: 1,600 to 2,900 feet.

Special attractions: Good fishing, several waterfalls (off the main trail though), and pretty streams.

Water availability: Salmon River and many small creeks.

Best season: Early spring through late fall.

For more information: Zigzag Ranger District, 70220 E. Highway 26, Zigzag, OR 97049; (503) 662-3191.

Permit: None.

Finding the trailhead: To reach the trailhead, drive to Zigzag, located off U.S. Highway 26, seventeen miles east of Sandy. Head south from town on Salmon River Road (later called Forest Road 2618) for 4.9 miles. At this point you'll see a bridge over the Salmon River. Park on the north side of the river at the signed trailhead.

The hike: Fishing is popular at the Salmon River where major runs of steelhead, coho and Chinook salmon return each year. Although the Salmon River National Recreation Trail is the most popular of seventy miles of trails that crisscross the area, you can still enjoy a bit of solitude if you travel several miles down the river.

Although the beginning and ending points of the trail vary by only 1,300 feet, you'll hike a lot of ups and down while traveling the Salmon River Trail 742. The first few miles of the trail are heavily-used, a fact which is quite noticeable as you hike through the temperate rain forest en route to the wilderness boundary at 1.9 miles.

As you hike, you'll notice spur trails leading down to the river. Some trails lead to waterfalls while others do not. Please use caution as the trails descend steep slopes. During the summer of 1989, a hiker died trying to view one of the waterfalls.

After passing Goat Creek at 4.8 miles, you'll see less people and perhaps more wildlife. Look for water ouzels along the river. Also known as dippers, these robin-size birds walk underwater looking for prey like bugs, larvae, and other tasty items.

Although this guide ends at the wilderness boundary near the twelve-mile mark, the trail does continue out of the wilderness to the trailhead at Mud Creek Road 2656-309, 1.8 miles farther.

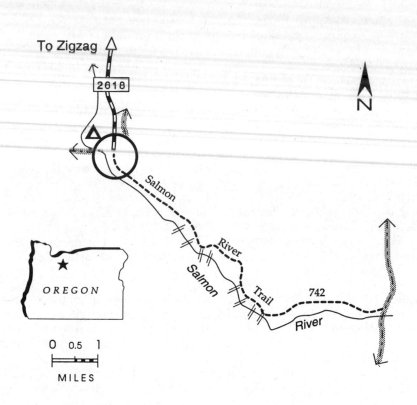

HIKE 63 *BADGER CREEK*

General description: A two- to three-day round-trip backpack in the Badger Creek Wilderness.

General location: About sixty-five miles southeast of Portland.

Maps: Flag Point 7.5-minute, Badger Lake 7.5-minute USGS quads.

Difficulty: Moderate.

Length: About eleven miles one way.

Elevations: 2,200 to 4,472 feet.

Special attractions: Solitude, an abundance of bird and animal life including wild turkeys, and forty-six species of butterflies.

Water availability: Badger Creek and other small creeks.

Best season: Portion of trail near Bonney Crossing is open in April. Badger

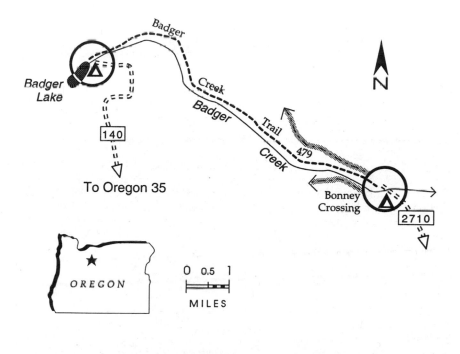

Badger

Creek

Badger   Trail

Creek

479

Badger
Lake

140

To Oregon 35

N

Bonney
Crossing

2710

★

OREGON

0   0.5   1

MILES

Lake area not accessible until mid- to late-June. The trail is usually open through November.

For more information: Barlow Ranger District, P.O. Box 67, Dufur, OR 97021; (541) 467-2291.

Permit: None.

Finding the trailhead: Two trailheads provide access. Those with a shuttle may want to begin at Badger Lake (the highest point) and hike southeast to Bonney Crossing. Reach the Bonney Crossing trailhead by driving a couple of miles past Bennett Pass, on Oregon 35, thirty-two miles south of the town of Hood River. Go southeast on Forest Road 48, later traveling Forest Roads 4810, 4811, and 2710 for twenty-two miles to Bonney Crossing. All the above roads are in fine condition.

The roads leading to Badger Lake, however, leave much to be desired. Reach the trailhead by driving 32.2 miles south of the town of Hood River, via Oregon 35. At Bennett Pass, turn left on Forest Road 3550 (a sign reads Road 550 instead of 3550), a narrow, primitive road with few turnouts. Reach a fork at 1.8 miles; head left. After 3.4 miles reach the junction of Forest Road 4860; make a right traveling past Camp Windy, a beautiful spot with a great view. Travel another 2.1 miles to another junction and make a left on Forest Road 140, going 3.4 miles to the trailhead.

The hike: This 24,000-acre preserve isn't big as far as wilderness areas go, but it is big on variety. Here, hikers enjoy the flora and fauna characteristic of both sides of the Cascade Mountains, although the preserve rests on the east crest.

Begin hiking signed Badger Creek Trail 479 (Badger Lake is about .2 mile to the south), entering the wilderness in .1 mile. Hike through dense forest crossing many streams along the way. This hike is very pleasant as you descend to a trail registration box at 10.8 miles. You'll exit the wilderness at eleven miles and reach the trailhead at Bonney Crossing just beyond.

HIKE 64 *LOOKOUT MOUNTAIN*

General description: A round-trip day hike in the Badger Creek Wilderness. A portion of the trail is barrier-free and accessible for wheelchair-bound hikers who can do a round-trip day hike.
General location: Approximately thirty-five miles south of Hood River.
Maps: Badger Lake 7.5-minute, Flag Point 7.5-minute USGS quads.
Difficulty: Moderate.
Length: About 2.5 miles one way.
Elevations: 6,000 to 6,525 feet.
Special attractions: Grand vistas and wildflowers galore.
Water availability: Senecal Spring.
Best season: July through October.
For more information: Barlow Ranger District, P.O. Box 67, Dufur, OR 97021; (541) 467-2291.
Permit: None.
Finding the trailhead: Reach the trailhead by driving 25.6 miles south from the town of Hood River on Oregon 35. At the Dufur Mill Road (Forest Road 44) junction make a left and go east for 3.8 miles to another junction. Make a right on High Prairie Road (Forest Road 4410), going 4.7 miles to a junction. Head left on Forest Road 4420, an unmaintained road leading .1 mile east to the trailhead.

The hike: From the top of Lookout Mountain you'll see most of the 24,000-acre Badger Creek Wilderness and points beyond. On a clear day you'll see much of the Cascade Range, from Washington's Mt. Rainier to Oregon's Three Sisters.

Begin hiking an old road through the High Prairie, a wonder of decorative wildflowers in July. Reach a fork at .8 mile and go left to a junction at 1.2 miles. Divide Trail 458 begins here. Head to the left and up 150 yards or so to the summit where you'll see to Washington's Mount St. Helens, Mt. Adams, and Mt. Rainier. Oregon's Mt. Hood seems but a stones throw away. Distant peaks include Mt. Jefferson and the Three Sisters.

Visit around late July and you'll see wildflowers blooming from the rocks

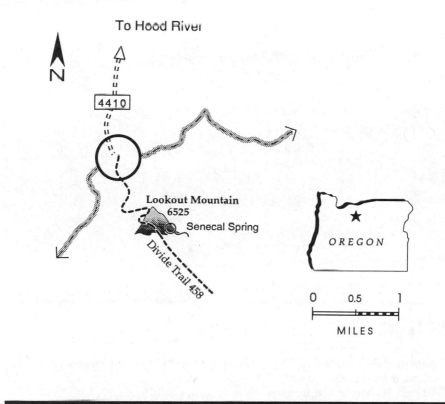

in this alpine zone where you'll feel as though you're on top of the world.

As long as you're up on the ridge, you'll probably want to continue your hike as there are some magnificent views and wildflowers galore along the way. Back at the junction, make a left, descending to another junction in .2 mile. Trail 458C leads to Senecal Spring, about 150 yards and 100 feet down. You'll hike the higher portion of the ridge until the 2.5-mile mark when you'll begin descending at a rapid rate.

View from the Divide Trail. Mt. Jefferson in back.

HIKE 65 *YOCUM RIDGE*

General description: A long round-trip day hike or a two-day round-trip backpack in the Mt. Hood Wilderness.
General location: Approximately fifty miles southeast of Portland.
Maps: Parkdale 7.5-minute USGS quad; Mt. Hood Wilderness map.
Difficulty: Moderate to difficult.
Length: About 7.6 miles one way.
Elevations: 2,800 to 6,200 feet.
Special attractions: Spectacular close-up views of Mt. Hood's glaciers, wildflowers, wildlife.
Water availability: See description.
Best season: July through October.
For more information: Zigzag Ranger District, Zigzag, OR 97049; (503) 622-3191.
Permit: None.
Finding the trailhead: Reach the trailhead from Zigzag, a tiny town off U.S. Highway 26. From town, go north on E. Lolo Pass Road for 4.1 miles. Make a right on Forest Road 1825 and drive 2.5 miles; make a left on Forest Road 100. Go 1.6 miles to the trailhead.

The hike: Begin hiking Ramona Falls Loop Trail 797 (either trail will do although this guide follows the first trail) after crossing the Sandy River. Reach the junction of the PCT at 1.6 miles. Turn left, reaching Ramona Falls at 2.1 miles.

You'll see another junction just past Ramona Falls. This is the remaining loop trail. Keep straight, ascending the PCT past a small stream and moss-covered rocks. Reach a junction at 2.9 miles.

Turn right on Yocum Ridge Trail 771, a pleasant hike through dense forest where the forest floor is often covered with rhododendrons. Cross the first of several small seasonal streams at 5.8 miles. If visiting just after snowmelt, you may see thousands of bright yellow avalanche lilies.

At about the 6.7-mile mark you'll see Mt. Jefferson to the south. There's a terrific view of the Reid Glacier and Sandy River drainage just up ahead.

You'll reach the end of the trail at 7.6 miles. There's a fantastic view into Sandy Glacier from this point and Mt. Hood, Oregon's highest peak at 11,237 feet, seems close enough to touch.

HIKE 65 *YOCUM RIDGE*

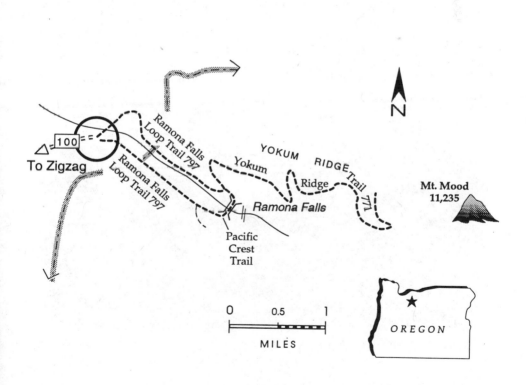

Hiker on Cooper Spur Trail. Mt. Hood in background.

HIKE 66 *COOPER SPUR*

General description: A round-trip day hike in the Mt. Hood Wilderness.
General location: Approximately thirty-five miles southwest of Hood River.
Maps: Parkdale 7.5-minute USGS quad; Mt. Hood Wilderness map.
Difficulty: Moderate to difficult.
Length: About four miles one way.
Elevations: 5,700 to 8,574 feet.
Special attractions: Outstanding close-up views of Mt. Hood and the Eliot and Newton Clark glaciers.
Water availability: None although snow may be available.
Best season: July through September.
For more information: Zigzag Ranger District, Zigzag, OR 97049; (503) 622-3191.
Permit: None.

HIKE 66 *COOPER SPUR*

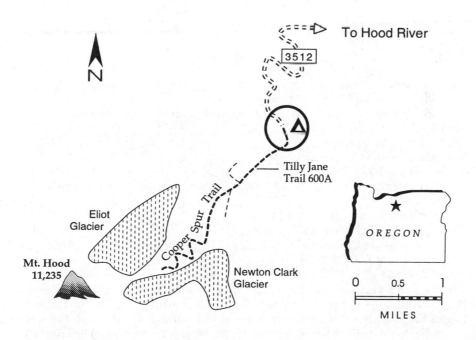

Finding the trailhead: To reach the trailhead, drive to the junction of Oregon 35 and Cooper Spur Road, located 22.5 miles south of Hood River and 16.2 miles northeast of Government Camp. Drive Cooper Spur Road 2.3 miles to Forest Road 35 12 (Cloud Cap Road); travel Forest Road 3512 to the trailhead, about ten miles distant. The trail begins at the Tilly Jane Campground.

The road leading to the trailhead is unique in that it passes through the Cloud Cap/Tilly Jane Historic District. A brochure, available at a road-side information board, describes how and when the road was made and mentions that the first motor vehicle to drive it was a 1907 Cadillac.

The hike: If, like me, you enjoy hiking above timberline, then you'll love hiking Cooper Spur. There are wonderful views into Eliot Glacier, the largest glacier on Mt. Hood, and the second largest glacier in the Beaver State.

Begin hiking Tilly Jane Trail 600A, hiking to the left and past the guard station. A sign leads the way past the American Legion Camp at .2 mile At less than a mile exit the trees and view Mt. Hood, and Washington's Mt. Rainier and Mt. Adams.

You'll reach a junction to the Timberline Trail at 1.2 miles. Continue straight up Cooper Spur Trail, past a shelter, eventually switchbacking up the ridge to the end of the trail.

Although it appears as though the 11,237-foot summit would be an easy scramble up the slope, it is not. The Forest Service highly recommends that climbers use an ice ax, rope, and crampons, when climbing the second most popular climbing route to the summit.

HIKE 67 *CEDAR SWAMP*

General description: A long round-trip day hike or a two-day round-trip backpack in the Columbia Wilderness.
General location: Approximately forty-four miles east of Portland.
Maps: Carson 7.5-minute USGS quad.
Difficulty: Moderate to difficult.
Length: About 7.7 miles one way.
Elevations: 160 to 2,800 feet
Special attractions: Old-growth forest including noble firs and western red cedar.
Water availability: See description.
Best season: May through November.
For more information: Columbia River Gorge National Scenic Area, 902 Wasco Avenue, Suite 200, Hood River, OR 97031.
Permit: None.
Finding the trailhead: The trailhead is located at the Columbia Gorge Work Center. To get there from the west, drive Interstate 84 to Cascade Locks Exit 44, about forty-four miles east of Portland. Go through town for one mile; head right at the fork. Pass under Interstate 84 and go left past the Oxbow Fish Hatchery to the work center, 2.3 miles from the fork. Turn right on Forest Road 215; reach the trailhead in .4 mile.

Those traveling westbound on Interstate 84 need to take the Forest Lane-

HIKE 67 *CEDAR SWAMP*

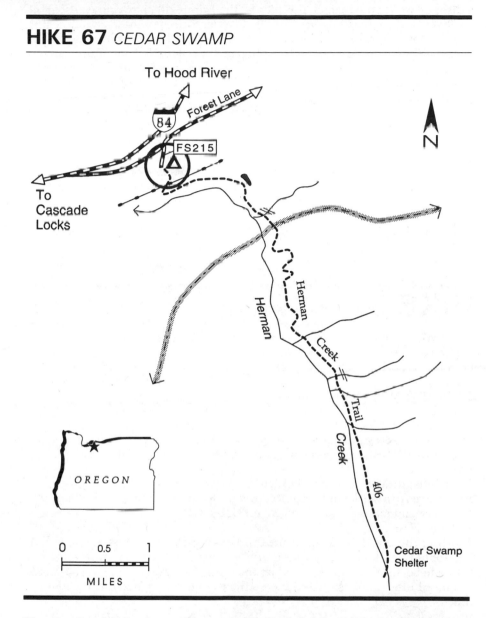

Herman Creek Exit, three miles east of Cascade Locks. Go under the freeway;
make a right on Forest Lane; go left on Forest Road 215 in .6 mile.

The hike: One of my personal favorites, Herman Creek Trail passes through
a lush forest of huge noble firs, western redcedar, Douglas-fir, and western
hemlock. Recognized as having "the best preserve of old-growth trees in the
Columbia Gorge Recreation Area," the trail doesn't actually reach the creek
until Cedar Swamp.

Poison oak is prevalent as you begin hiking Herman Creek Trail 406, but it disappears as you ascend. You'll cross the Bonneville powerline easement at .3 mile, then reach a junction at .7 mile. Another intersection is just ahead; turn right on the old road.

Reach the Gorton Creek Trail junction at 1.4 miles. Herman Camp, an old camp, is here and there's suppose to be a spring near by, but I never saw it. One piece of literature claims it is 500 feet northwest of the camp, the Forest Service claims it is southwest of it.

The road narrows to a standard trail at the two-mile mark. Shortly thereafter, pass Falls Creek Waterfall, a beautiful falls cascading down basalt cliffs. Enter the wilderness at 2.8 miles, crossing Camp Creek just beyond.

About five miles into the hike, you'll reach another falls at Slide Creek. Cross several more creeks before reaching Cedar Swamp Shelter at 7.3 miles. The shelter isn't much to speak of. Built by the Forest Service and Boy Scouts Troop 607, many blowdowns caused its demise in January 1990.

Ancient cedars surround the shelter and the trail from here to Herman Creek at 7.7 miles. Just past the creek there are some magnificent noble firs.

HIKE 68 *TANNER BUTTE*

General description: A long round-trip day hike or a two-day round-trip backpack in the Columbia Wilderness.

General location: Approximately forty miles east of Portland.

Maps: Tanner Butte 7.5-minute USGS quad.

Difficulty: Moderate to difficult.

Length: About 7.2 miles one way.

Elevations: 1,100 to 4,500 feet.

Special attractions: Fantastic views, wildlife, wildflowers, solitude.

Water availability: Several streams in the beginning of the hike, Dublin Lake.

Best season: Mid-June through late October.

For more information: Columbia River Gorge National Scenic Area, 902 Wasco Avenue, Suite 200, Hood River, OR 97031.

Permit: None.

Finding the trailhead: Reach the trailhead by driving Interstate 84 to Exit 40, about forty miles east of Portland, 3 .2 miles west of the small town of Cascade Locks. Go to the left and up the unmarked gravel road. A sign reads "Tanner Butte - 2 miles." Continue up the road to the signed trailhead in 2.1 miles.

The hike: This trail provides something most hikers crave—solitude. Hikers enter the 39,000-acre preserve via Tanner Butte Trail 401. Climb a steep grade through thick forest then the trail angle lessens to moderate. Cross several streams and pass a stream before reaching the Wauna Viewpoint Trail 402 junction at 2.1 miles. There's a good view 1.8 miles down the trail.

Enter the wilderness at 2.4 miles, continuing along the ridge to 4.3 miles and the Dublin Lake Trail 401B. A very steep trail leads .4 mile to the lake.

HIKE 68 *TANNER BUTTE*

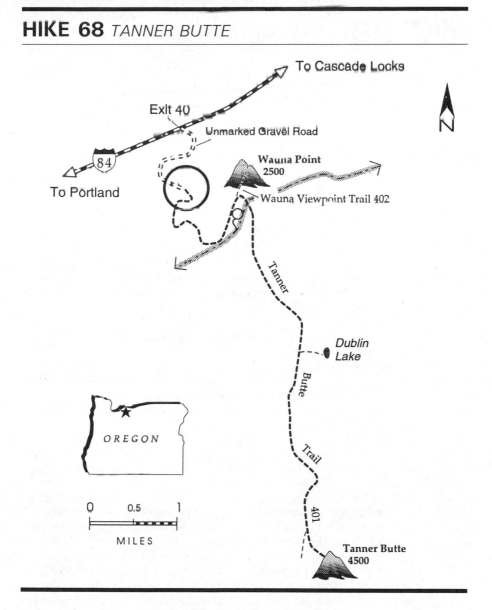

To Cascade Locks

Exit 40

Unmarked Gravel Road

84

To Portland

Wauna Point
2500

Wauna Viewpoint Trail 402

Tanner

Butte

Trail

401

Dublin
Lake

Tanner Butte
4500

OREGON

0   0.5   1

MILES

As you progress along the Tanner Butte Trail, it will widen from a standard trail to an old road lined with a variety of wildflowers in the proper season. At 6.7 miles you'll come to the west slope of Tanner Butte and a sign "Scramble Trail."

The unmaintained trail leads through thick huckleberry bushes making it difficult to follow at times. There is some flagging, however. Just aim for the summit and there should be no problem in finding it.

From atop Tanner Butte see Mounts Hood and Jefferson, and Washington's Mount St. Helens, Adams, and Rainier.

HIKE 69 *NEAHKANIE MOUNTAIN*

General description: A round-trip day hike at Oswald West State Park.
General location: Approximately thirty-nine miles south of Astoria, 100 miles west of Portland.
Maps: Nehalem 7.5-minute USGS quad.
Difficulty: Moderate.
Length: About 1.5 miles one way.
Elevations: 720 to 1,631 feet.
Special attractions: Magnificent views, some old-growth trees, wildlife.
Water availability: None.
Best season: Year-round.
For more information: Oregon State Parks and Recreation Division, 525 Trade St. S.E., Salem, OR 97310; (503) 378-6305.
Permit: None.
Finding the trailhead: From the small town of Manzanita (all services), about thirty-nine miles south of Astoria, go north on U.S. Highway 101 for 1.5 miles. Make a right on a gravel road marked with a "hiking trail" sign and reach the signed trailhead in .4 mile.

The hike: Mention Neahkahnie Mountain—known in legends as "Home of the Gods"—to some people and images of buried treasure light faces. Tales of riches, hidden by Spanish sailors in the early 1700's, even prompt some modern-day treasure hunters to search for the valuable cargo. Skeptics claim the treasure may be in the sea or buried deep within the mountain for the mountain has obviously shifted a great deal in the past 200 years. Still, it doesn't stop the searching.

Whether you're into treasures or you just enjoy moderate hikes with great views and the chance of observing elk, then this trail is for you. Located in the Oswald West State Park, there is camping nearby at both Oswald West and Nehalem Bay State Parks.

Begin climbing the moderate grade, switchbacking up through the forest where giant spruce live. An occasional open slope provides a view to the south.

Reach a saddle at one mile. Cross an old road and continue straight on the signed trail which leads the way to Short Sand Beach in 2.5 miles.

Now the trail traverses the north side of the mountain, reaching a point near the summit at 1.5 miles. Scramble up the short, steep trail for 100 feet or so to a wonderful view of the Pacific and points to the south.

From here you can return to the trailhead or continue down to U.S. Highway 101 near Short Sand Beach.

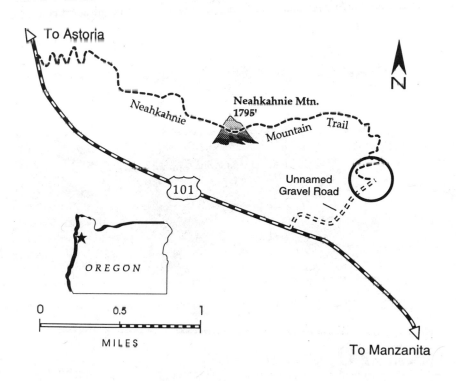

To Astoria

Neahkahnie

Neahkahnie Mtn.
1795'

Mountain Trail

Unnamed
Gravel Road

101

OREGON

0   0.5   1

MILES

To Manzanita

Munson Creek; fall leaves.

HIKE 70 *MUNSON FALLS*

General description: A short day hike to a view of Munson Falls.
General location: Approximately seven miles south of Tillamook.
Maps: Tillamook 15-minute USGS quad.
Difficulty: Easy.
Length: About .2 mile one way.
Elevations: 50 feet.
Special attractions: View of Munson Falls, the highest waterfall in the Coast Range.
Water availability: Munson Creek.
Best season: Year-round.
For more information: Tillamook Chamber of Commerce, 3705 Hwy. 101 N, Tillamook, OR 97141; (503) 842-7525.
Permit: None.
Finding the trailhead: From downtown Tillamook (all services available), home of the famous Tillamook Cheese Factory, go south on U.S. Highway 101 for 7.2 miles. Make a left on a signed roadway leading to Munson Falls. The paved road turns to gravel as it continues one mile to a fork; go left following the signs then make a right at another fork in .5 mile. Reach the trailhead and a picnic area (pit toilet, picnic tables) 1.6 miles from U.S. Highway 101.

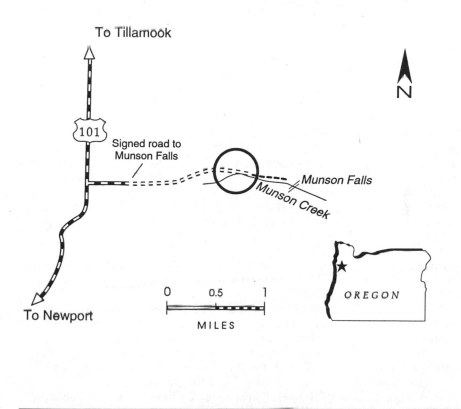

Please note: The Tillamook County Road Department asks that those pulling trailers refrain from driving to the Munson Creek Falls trailhead. There is absolutely no room for turning them around.

The hike: Munson Falls is not only the highest waterfall in the Coast Range, it's easily accessible. Dropping 266 feet over rugged cliffs, the creek becomes passive after the drop, with tiny pools begging to be explored. In fall, colorful maple leaves decorate the scene. A short trail leads to a point near the falls making this a perfect hike for those with children.

There is one trail leading to Munson Creek Falls, although you'll see evidence of another trail—The Upper Trail—that is closed indefinitely. A landslide occurred in April of 1991, wiping out the trail and partially rerouting the lower trail. Because the Upper Trail is so insecure, there are no plans to reopen it at this time.

HIKE 71 NIAGARA FALLS / PHEASANT CREEK FALLS

General description: A short day hike in the Siuslaw National Forest.
General location: About fifty miles northwest of Salem.
Maps: Niagara Creek 7.5-minute USGS quad.
Difficulty: Moderate.
Length: Approximately one mile one way.
Elevations: 1,400 to 950 feet.
Special attractions: Two lovely waterfalls, solitude.
Water availability: Niagara Creek, Pheasant Creek.
Best season: All year, although upper elevations may be closed by occasional snow.
For more information: Siuslaw National Forest, Hebo Ranger District, 31525 Hwy. 22, Hebo, OR 97122, (503) 392-3161
Permit: None.
Finding the trailhead: From Beaver, a small town with a market, deli, and gas, located off U.S. Highway 101, go east on paved Nestucca River Road. A sign points the way to Blaine.

At 11.6 miles make a right on Forest Road 8533 which turns to gravel. Make another right on Forest Road 131 in 4.2 miles, reaching the trailhead in .7 mile.

The hike: This is a great hike for the entire family. If Mom or Dad carry along a picnic lunch, the clan can feast while sitting at a picnic table resting right in front of Niagara Falls.

Although the falls are a lovely spot year round, they are best visited in the winter when there is a greater stream flow. Visit in late summer and you may find, like we did, only a trickle.

It's a moderate descent (trail open to hikers only) with some occasional steep grades. You'll pass through thick forest where some enormous Douglas-fir trees abound. Red alder add color in the fall.

You'll cross an unnamed creek (via wooden bridges) on several occasions en route.

Pass Pheasant Creek Falls, a gentle cascade, just before reaching eighty-foot high Niagara Falls. Both falls tumble over rugged cliffs, smoothed by a multitude of ever-present water droplets.

HIKE 71 *NIAGRA FALLS/PHEASANT CREEK FALLS*

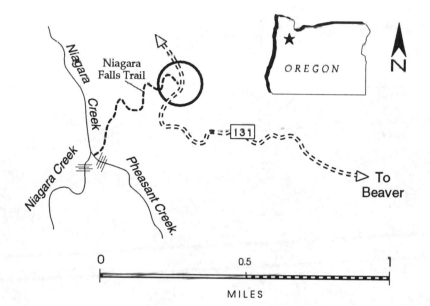

HIKE 72 *HARTS COVE*

General description: A long day hike in the Siuslaw National Forest.
General location: About six miles north of Lincoln City, sixty miles west of Salem.
Maps: Hebo 15-minute USGS quad.
Difficulty: Moderate to difficult.
Length: Approximately 2.9 miles one way.
Elevations: 1,200 to 100 feet.
Special attractions: Excellent view of Harts Cove and the mighty Pacific; animal life including migrating gray whales and sea lions.
Water availability: Cliff Creek, Chitwood Creek.
Best season: All year.

View to the south from bluff near Harts Cove.

For more information: Siuslaw National Forest, Hebo Ranger District, 31525 Hwy. 22, Hebo, OR 97122; (503) 392-3161.

Permit: None, but the trail is closed seasonally form January 1 through July 15 to protect sesistive species habitat. Hiking is permitted from July 16 through December 31.

Finding the trailhead: From Lincoln City, where all amenities are accessible, go north on U.S. Highway 101 for a bout six miles. Make a left on Cascade Head Road (Forest Road 1861), taking it to the end in four miles.

The hike: This is an excellent hike, although you should be warned about the first half mile—it's a very steep descent, about twenty to thirty percent. Afterwards, though, the trail descends at a mostly easy grade to a meadow overlooking the Pacific and Harts Cove. You will enjoy looking for whales and

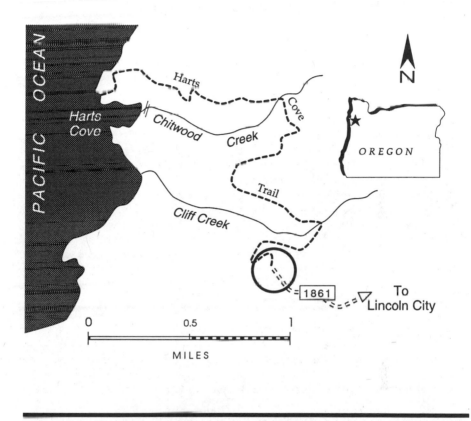

love watching sea lions, listening to their incessant barking.

You drive through the Cascade Head Research Area where interpretative signs inform you of the processes that formed this area. After a fire, bare soil predominates. As time passes, red alder takes hold, only to be bumped out by spruce and later western hemlock. It's no surprise that with over 100 inches of rain annually and a nine-month growing season, vegetation grows quite rapidly.

Encompassing more than 9,700 acres of headland and surrounding area, the Cascade Head Scenic Research Area was established in 1974. A study area for many years, it boasts 378 species of wildlife. Other study areas include the Cascade Head Experimental Forest, established in 1934, and the Neskowin Crest Research Natural Area, founded in 1941.

Harts Cove Trail is closed to motor vehicles, horses and pack animals. As mentioned previously, it's a steep descent via switchback, traveling through a forest of alder and young spruce. Look for trilliums in the spring/summer. At .8 mile cross Cliff Creek via a bridge.

Now the grade is gentle with easy ups and downs. The forest is primarily mature spruce, with 250-year-old trees in evidence.

Now and just prior to this point you'll no doubt hear many sea lions resting in a cove to the south. Just ahead there's a bench where you can sit and enjoy the view to the north of Harts Cove.

Continue on, traveling the Chitwood Creek drainage to the east. Cross another bridge, this one over Chitwood Creek, at two miles. Head back to the west.

Reach a large hillside meadow at 2.7 miles. There's a nice view from here, but an even better one if you head down the slope (blanketed with wildflowers in the spring/summer) to the south. Reach the bluff edge at 2.9 miles.

From this point you'll view Chitwood Falls as it tumbles into Harts Cove. This is also an excellent spot from which to observe sea lions in the cove to the south. To the north see Cape Kiwanda.

If time permits, look for migrating gray whales. These behemoths swim more than 10,000 miles each year, traveling from their rich feeding grounds in the Arctic to their breeding and birthing grounds in the lagoons off Mexico's Baja California. December and January mark the best times for viewing the southward migration, while late February and March are best for the northward migration.

While you're at Harts Cove enjoying the view and wildlife, imagine living in such a paradise. In 1916, Charles Hart, a lifelong bachelor, did just that. He resided in a cabin perched high atop the meadow near Harts Cove, running cattle and growing vegetables. Each day Hart, a school teacher, hiked six miles one way to the small town of Otis where he taught the local children in a one-room cabin.

HIKE 73 *JOHNSON CREEK*

General description: A one-way or round-trip day hike in the Siskiyou National Forest.

General location: About thirty-six miles east of Port Orford (nineteen airline miles).

Maps: Agness 15-minute, Powers 15-minute USGS quads.

Difficulty: Moderate.

Length: Approximately 2.5 miles one way.

Elevations: 1,040 to 2,240 feet.

Special attractions: Solitude, wildlife, wildflowers, old-growth forest.

Water availability: See text.

Best season: All year.

For more information: Siskiyou National Forest, Powers Ranger District, Powers, OR 97466; (541) 439-3011.

Permit: None.

Finding the trailhead: To reach the southern trailhead, head north from Port Orford (all services), located on U.S. Highway 101. Go three miles on U.S. Highway 101 then head east on County Road 208 (Elk River Road) which eventually turns into Forest Road 5325. The paved road follows the scenic Elk River, often bordering the south edge of the Grassy Knob Wilderness.

HIKE 73 *JOHNSON CREEK*

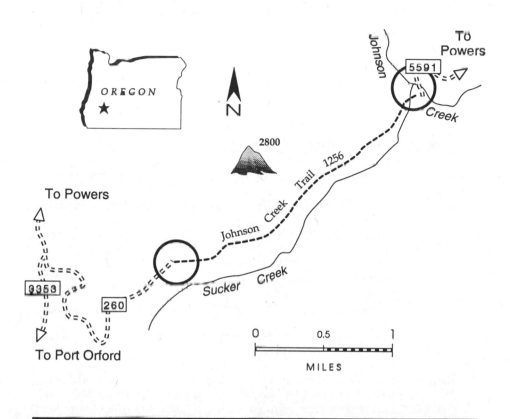

Pass several free campgrounds as you travel east. You'll come to the Butler Campground at 18.5 miles; now Forest Road 5325 turns from paved to a well-maintained gravel road and heads away from the Elk River. Continue another nine miles to a junction; go left on Forest Road 3353. Continue another 7.6 miles to Forest Road 260, a spur road, heading to the right and down to the trailhead in 1.6 miles.

The Hike: Johnson Creek is a terrific hike where you're bound to enjoy solitude. Hike through an old-growth forest of Douglas-fir and cedar, an area ablaze with rhododendron blossoms in the spring/early summer. If have access to a car shuttle, begin at the south and upper end of the trail, descending to the north end.

Access to the northern trailhead is via Powers, about twenty miles to the north. From Powers, go south on County Road 219 to Forest Service Road 33. Head west on Forest Road 3353 then south on Forest Road 5591.

From Forest Road 260, descend via Johnson Creek Trail 1256, a hiker's only trail. Vegetation is dense and old-growth forest pleasant as you follow the Sucker Creek drainage, crossing tiny creeks at .5, 1.4, 1.9, and 2.1 miles.

The trail descends at a moderate grade for the most part, although you'll drop at a steep grade when you first begin your hike. Fortunately, the steep grade is short-lived.

Ford Sucker Creek (it can be hazardous after heavy rains) using caution, then continue along the creek bottom for 100 yards before hiking up on level ground, reaching the trailhead in another 100 feet or so. There's an unimproved campsite here.

If you walk onto Forest Road 5591, you'll see where Sucker Creek merges into Johnson Creek, your first glimpse of the creek for which this trail was named.

HIKE 74 *IRON MOUNTAIN*

General description: A one-way or round-trip day hike in the Siskiyou National Forest.
General location: About thirty miles east of Port Orford (eighteen airline miles).
Maps: Agness 15-minute USGS quads.
Difficulty: Moderate.
Length: Approximately 2.7 miles one way.
Elevations: 3,400 to 4,064 feet.
Special attractions: Solitude, wildlife, wildflowers, grand views.
Water availability: None.
Best season: All year.
For more information: Siskiyou National Forest, Powers Ranger District, Powers, OR 97466; (541) 439-3011.
Permit: None.
Finding the trailhead: The southern trailhead (and starting point for this guide) is accessible from Port Orford (all services). Go north on U.S. Highway 101 for three miles; turn right on County Road 208 (Elk River Road) which turns into Forest Road 5325 along the way. Pass several free campgrounds before the paved road turns to well-maintained gravel at 18.5 miles. Continue another 11.7 miles on Forest Road 5325 to the trailhead.

The northern entry is about thirty miles south of Powers via County Road 219 and Forest Roads 33 and 3347. If you're only interested in hiking the high points of Iron Mountain, this is your best bet. You can hike from here to the site of an old lookout, about two miles to the south, always remaining near the 4,000 foot level.

The hike: This trail can be reached from two different trailheads, one in the south and one in the north, thus it makes a good trail for those wanting to hike one-way, returning via car shuttle. The trail is also easy enough to hike in both directions and still have energy to spare.

From Forest Road 5325, begin hiking Iron Mountain Trail 1265, a trail open to hikers, bikers, and horseback riders. The trail is actually an old cat road which climbs the Port Orford cedar/white fir slope then follows the ridge to Forest Road 3347, the northern trailhead.

View to the north from Iron Mountain.

Climb moderately to .7 mile and a spur trail leading about .1 mile to a grand vista atop Iron Mountain. The site used to be a Forest Service lookout. Today it makes a great spot for a picnic with a 360-degree view for dessert.

Continue north on the main trail, looking for signs of bear and other animal life along the way. We saw plenty of bear scat and many deer tracks. Numerous rhododendron and azalea plants line the trail, producing a colorful display in the spring/early summer. Occasionally there is a view of the surrounding countryside.

Reach some sort of communications tower at 2.6 miles then continue on to the trailhead at 2.7 miles.

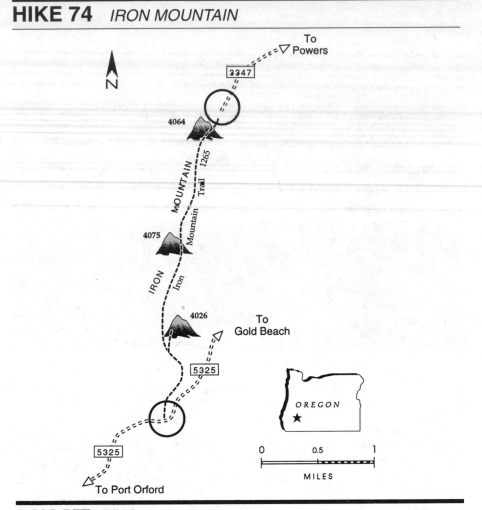

HIKE 75 *BARKLOW MOUNTAIN*

General description: A short day hike in the Siskiyou National Forest.

General location: About thirty-seven miles east of Port Orford (eighteen airline miles).

Maps: Agness 15-minute, Powers 15-minute USGS quads.

Difficulty: Easy to moderate.

Length: Approximately .7 mile one way.

Elevations: 3,600 to 3,579 feet.

Special attractions: This trail provides a short, steep workout with opportunities for viewing wildlife. There's a wonderful view of the Siskiyou Mountains from the summit, where you'll see to the Pacific as well. Solitude is another plus.

Water availability: None.

Best season: All year.

For more information: Siskiyou National Forest, Powers Ranger District, Powers, OR 97466; (541) 439-3011.

Permit: None.

Finding the trailhead: About three miles north of Port Orford (all services), located on U.S. Highway 101, go east on County Road 208 (Elk River Road) which turns into Forest Road 5325 along the way. This paved road traces the scenic Elk River, often bordering the south edge of the Grassy Knob Wilderness.

Pass several free campgrounds as you travel east. You'll come to the Butler Campground at 18.5 miles; now Forest Road 5325 turns from paved to a well-maintained gravel road. Continue another nine miles to a junction; go left on Forest Road 3353. Continue another 9.8 miles to the trailhead which is on the left.

HIKE 75 *BARKLOW MOUNTAIN*

The hike: Begin hiking Barklow Mountain Trail 1258, a trail open to hiker's only, passing through the trees, traveling a pretty steep grade for the first mile or so.

The trail passes through typical second-growth forest. Look for deer, grouse, stellar jays, and other animal species along the way.

You'll come to a junction just short of a mile. Keep right on Trail 1258, going up to the site of an old lookout in another 0.1 mile. From here, there's nearly a 360-degree view of the surrounding area.

The trail leading straight at the junction is not maintained. According to the Forest Service, the trail leads to an old shelter which has not been used in some time.

RESOURCES

Local Hiking Clubs and Conservation Organizations:

Portland Audubon Society, 5151 N.W. Cornell Rd., Portland, OR 97210; (503) 292-6855.

The Wildlife Society, Rt. 5, Box 325, Corvallis, OR 97330; (503) 757-4186.

American Hiking Society, 1015 31st St., N.W., Washington, DC 20007; (703) 385-3252.

Izaak Walton League, P.O. Box 517, Hines, OR 97738; (503) 573-2997.

Desert Trail Association, P.O. Box 589, Burns, OR 97720.

Oregon Natural Resources Council, 1161 Lincoln St., Eugene, OR 97401; (503) 334-0675.

Further Reading:

Aitkenhead, Donna, *Southern Oregon Wilderness Areas.* The Touchstone Press: Beaverton, Oregon, 1988.

Aitkenhead, Donna, *Eastern Oregon Wilderness Areas.* The Touchstone Press: Beaverton, Oregon, 1990.

Aitkenhead, Donna, *Central Oregon Wilderness Areas.* The Touchstone Press: Beaverton, Oregon, 1991.

Aitkenhead, Donna, *Northern Oregon Wilderness Areas.* The Touchstone Press: Beaverton, Oregon, 1992. (Due out in April, 1992.)

The above titles are available from Frank Amato Publications, Portland, Oregon.

Barstad, Fred, *Hiking Oregon's Eagle Cap Wilderness.* Falcon Press: Helena, Montana, 1996

Lowe, Don and Roberta, *Sixty Hiking Trails: Central Oregon Cascades.* The Touchstone Press: Beaverton, Oregon, 1978.

Lowe, Don and Roberta, *Sixty-two Hiking Trails: Northern Oregon Cascades.* The Touchstone Press: Beaverton, Oregon, 1979.

Meissner, Virginia, *Day Hikes in Central Oregon.* Meissner Books: Bend, Oregon, 1981.

Meissner, Virginia, *Hiking Central Oregon and Beyond.* Meissner Books: Bend, Oregon, 1987.

Ostertag, Rhonda, *Fifty Hikes in Oregon's Coast Range and Siskiyous.* The Mountaineers Books: Seattle, Washington, 1989.

Sullivan, William L., *Exploring Oregon's Wild Areas: A Guide for Hikers, Backpackers, X-C Skiers & Paddlers.* Mountaineers: Seattle, Washington, 1988.

Sullivan, William L., *Listening for Coyote: A Walk Across Oregon's Wilderness.* H. Holt & Co: New York, New York, 1990.

Wallowa Resource Council Staff, *Hiking the High Wallowas: Eighteen Hikes in Northeast Oregon.* Pika Oregon, Enterprise, Oregon, 1988.

Williams, Paul M., *Oregon Coast Hikes.* The Mountaineers Books: Seattle, Washington, 1985.

Finding Maps:

Wilderness maps are available from the district managing each wilderness area. Addresses and phone numbers of the managing agencies are provided with the statistics on each hike.

Maps for trails found on land other than designated wilderness are sometimes available from the governing agency, but these are not always topographic maps. For topo maps contact the United States Geological Survey (USGS), Western Distribution Branch, Box 25286, Denver Federal Center, Denver, CO 80225. Some specialty backpacking stores and sporting goods stores also carry the maps.

ABOUT THE AUTHOR

Donna Ikenberry and her Samoyed from Dead Horse Rim.

Donna Ikenberry is a writer/photographer who travels year-round. Calling a 30 ft. fifth wheel trailer "home" for the nearly thirteen years, she says Oregon is her favorite parking space.

She has written four other hiking guides to Oregon: *Southern Oregon Wilderness Areas, Eastern Oregon Wilderness Areas, Central Oregon Wilderness Areas,* and *Northern Oregon Wilderness Areas.* An avid bicyclist, she has authoured two bicycling guidebooks, *Bicycling the Atlantic Coast,* and *Bicycling Coast to Coast.*

In addition to books, Donna has had more than 300 articles published on various topics. Also, hundreds of her photographs have graced the covers and pages of many magazines, books, postcards, advertisements, posters, and calendars.

HIKING NOTES

HIKING NOTES

HIKING NOTES

HIKING NOTES

HIKING NOTES

FALCON GUIDES HIKE it

■ *To order any of these books, or to request an expanded list of available titles, including guides for viewing wildlife, birding, scenic driving, or rockhounding, please call 1-800-582-2665, or write to Falcon, PO Box 1718, Helena, MT 59624.*